Lecture Notes in Computer Science   1859

Edited by G. Goos, J. Hartmanis, and J. van Leeuwen

Springer
Berlin
Heidelberg
New York
Barcelona
Hong Kong
London
Milan
Paris
Tokyo

Marcus Jürgens

Index Structures
for Data Warehouses

 Springer

Series Editors

Gerhard Goos, Karlsruhe University, Germany
Juris Hartmanis, Cornell University, NY, USA
Jan van Leeuwen, Utrecht University, The Netherlands

Author

Marcus Jürgens
Freie Universität Berlin
Fachbereich für Mathematik und Informatik, Institut für Informatik
Takustraße 9, 14195 Berlin, Germany
E-mail: marcus.juergens@gmx.de

Cataloging-in-Publication Data applied for

Die Deutsche Bibliothek - CIP-Einheitsaufnahme

Jürgens, Marcus:
Index structures for data warehouses / Marcus Jürgens. - Berlin ; Heidelberg ;
New York ; Barcelona ; Hong Kong ; London ; Milan ; Paris ; Singapore ;
Tokyo : Springer, 2002
  (Lecture notes in computer science ; 1859)
  Zugl.: Berlin, Freie Univ., Diss., 2000
  ISBN 3-540-43368-6

CR Subject Classification (1998): H.3.1, H.2.7, H.3, H.2

ISSN 0302-9743
ISBN 3-540-43368-6 Springer-Verlag Berlin Heidelberg New York

Springer-Verlag Berlin Heidelberg New York
a member of BertelsmannSpringer Science+Business Media GmbH

http://www.springer.de

© Springer-Verlag Berlin Heidelberg 2002

Typesetting: Camera-ready by author, data conversion by Boller Mediendesign
Printed on acid-free paper   SPIN: 10846408   06/3142   5 4 3 2 1 0

Preface

This thesis investigates which index structures support query processing in typical data warehouse environments most efficiently. Data warehouse applications differ significantly from traditional transaction-oriented operational applications. Therefore, the techniques applied in transaction-oriented systems cannot be used in the context of data warehouses and new techniques must be developed.

The thesis shows that the time complexity for the computation of *optimal* tree-based index structures prohibits its use in real world applications. Therefore, we *improve* heuristic techniques (*e. g.* R^*-tree) to process range queries on aggregated data more efficiently. Experiments show the benefits of this approach for different kinds of typical data warehouse queries. Performance models *estimate* the behavior of standard index structures and the behavior of the extended index structures. We introduce a new model that considers the distribution of data. We show experimentally that the new model is more precise than other models known from literature. Two techniques *compare* two tree-based index structures with two bitmap indexing techniques. The performance of these index structures depends on a set of different parameters. Our results show which index structure performs most efficiently depending on the parameters.

Acknowledgements

I am very grateful to have had the opportunity to write my Ph. D. Thesis under the supervision of Professor Hans-Joachim Lenz who brought the area of data warehouses to my attention. In countless meetings he gave me helpful feedback. I would like to thank Professor Heinz Schweppe for his constructive suggestions and the invitation to cooperate with the database group at the Freie Universität Berlin. Professor Freytag supported me with beneficial ideas and outstanding comments.

The graduate school in Distributed Information Systems would not be possible in this efficient form without its speaker Professor Oliver Günther. His commitment gives this school a constructive and pleasant environment.

I would like to express my thanks to all members of database groups participating in this graduate school for their interesting and encouraging talks and discussions. In particular, I am grateful for the constructive discussions with Agnès Voisard and Annika Hinze. The *Deutsche Forschungsgemeinschaft (DFG)* supported me as a fellowship recipient. Professor Joseph Bronstad and Leslie Hazelwood did not give up trying to correct my English.

Contents

1 Introduction

During the last decades many companies have invested much effort in the area of information technology. Most of the effort went into the optimization of transaction-oriented operational systems. The main goal of these systems is to transport data as quickly and as cost efficiently as possible. Operational systems model and represent the dynamic behavior of processes. In this area much research has been conducted and sophisticated solutions have been developed. Typical operational systems store data about customers and transactions in databases. Database management systems (DBMSs) have been developed to support the processing of transactions on this data efficiently.

But apart from the use in operational systems, valuable strategic information is also hidden in the operational data. The extraction of this information by analysts may help companies to operate more efficiently. In particular, complex analytical queries on historic data over extended time periods are useful. Since the operational systems cannot deal with additional work load caused by complex analytical queries, the data has to be transfered from the operational systems to some other system dedicated only for analysis. These systems are called *Data Warehouses*.

Usually the data for these systems is stored with DBMSs. Relational DBMS (RDBMS) are the best understood technique to deal with large data sets. However they were not primarily designed for these new kinds of data and applications. There are three major differences between transaction-oriented operational systems and data warehouse systems:

- Size of the data: Fast access to GB ($\approx 10^9$ bytes) or TB ($\approx 10^{12}$ bytes) of data is crucial in providing interactive decision support. For these large sets, table scans, even on parallel systems, should be avoided whenever possible.
- Dynamics of data: In a typical data warehouse, data is inserted, but exceptionally updated or deleted. Furthermore, insertion only takes place at certain time windows when the system is not accessible for the analysts. Outside these time windows, analysts use the system only for reading data. This strategy is typical for *read-mostly* environments.
- Type of queries: In data warehouse and in operational systems different queries are processed. Typical queries in an operational system access data on a very detailed level, such as the *balance of a specific bank account*.

Typical queries in data warehouse environments calculate aggregated data over large sets of data, such as *sum of sales on product groups for some time period*. Therefore, the access to aggregated data over large sets of data has to be supported efficiently.

Since data warehouses are used for *interactive* decision support and not in batch mode, the response time of queries should be as short as possible. The analysts submit any query in ad-hoc fashion against the data warehouse. Different techniques are applied to reduce the query execution time. One technique to increase the performance is the use of *index structures*. Index structures avoid full table scans if only a small fraction of the stored tuples is used for result computation. Different methods, such as *B*-trees, have been investigated in large detail for operational databases during the last decades, but not for data warehouse systems. Therefore, the research question of this thesis is: What index structures are best suited for data warehouse systems?

1.1 Goals

This thesis investigates which index structures are well suited for data warehouse systems. We provide in detail answers to the following four questions:

1. What should an *optimal* index structure for data warehouses look like; *e. g.*, how can *optimality* be defined and what is the time complexity to calculate such an *optimal* solution?
   We describe one approach which guarantees finding an *optimal* index structure by mapping the problem of finding an *optimal* index structure to a Mixed Integer Problem (MIP) and solving the MIP with scientific standard software.
2. How can existing index structures be *improved* to support typical data warehouse queries more efficiently?
   We discuss in detail an extension of index structures where aggregated data is materialized in the inner nodes of an index structures. This extension can be applied to most tree-based index structures.
3. How can the performance of such extended structures be *predicted*?
   We extend performance models known from literature to model the behavior of the structure with aggregated data in the inner nodes. Furthermore, we develop a new model which considers the actual distribution of data and the distribution of queries.
4. How can different index structures be *compared*?
   We describe two approaches for comparing index structures. We apply these techniques and present results of comparisons of different index structures. Especially the time/space tradeoff and the evolving technology for secondary memories are considered in our comparisons.

1.2 Outline

Synopses of Chapter 2 through Chapter 8 follow below:

Chapter 2. Data warehouse systems, as mentioned before, differ greatly from traditional transaction-oriented database systems. This chapter describes the major differences between the two types of systems. Operational systems do not efficiently support the extraction of information through complex analytical queries. Data warehouse systems need to be designed and implemented which support the decision making process. We describe the specific properties of these data warehouse systems. The chapter also discusses several approaches on how to accelerate query processing in a typical data warehouse environment.

Chapter 3. Among the most important properties of DBMSs is the ability to handle large amounts of data. Different technologies are used to store and retrieve this data efficiently. Large sets of data do not fit into main memory and, therefore, are stored on secondary memory. Fast accesses to the data have to be provided to retrieve the data. The mechanics of the disks influence the performance of the index structures. In order to process queries efficiently, different access structures have been developed in traditional academic research. This chapter presents different kinds of structures that organize multidimensional data efficiently. We focus on the R-tree family, on the multi-component equality encoded indexes, and on the range encoded bitmap indexes because of their flexibilities.

Chapter 4. Since there is a strict separation of insert operations and read operations in data warehouses, one method of increasing the query processing speed is to invest more effort in organizing the data such that read operations perform quickly. We describe an approach for finding optimal index structures. We first define optimality, and then solve the problem of computing an optimal structure by transforming the problem into a Mixed Integer Problem (MIP). This MIP is solved with scientific standard software. Experiments show a serve problem: The time complexity of the MIP increases exponentially with the number of tuples and the number of clusters. Because of this exponential growth, this approach is in general infeasible. Therefore, in the following chapters of this thesis, we apply heuristic techniques for improving index structure for data warehousing. One application of computing optimal index structures with a MIP is to evaluate for small data sets how closely the heuristic approaches attain their optimum.

Chapter 5. The results of typical queries in data warehouse systems are aggregated data from large sets of data and not values of specific tuples. To support such queries we examine a technique where we materialize aggregated data in the inner nodes of a tree-based index structure. This data could also be calculated from data stored in leaf nodes, but the access to the aggregated data in the inner nodes is certainly faster than accesses to successor nodes.

This concept of aggregated data in the inner nodes is generic and is applicable to most tree-based index structures. We show how to modify algorithms to maintain and to use the aggregated data. In particular we modify the R^*-tree in such a way which leads to the so called R_a^*-tree. We present results of experiments comparing the R_a^*-tree and the R^*-tree. Results show that the performance of queries on aggregated data is significantly increased by using the extended structure.

Chapter 6. DBMSs can create different index structures on the same table. In order to choose the fastest index structure, it is desirable to have analytical models which predict the performance. For some index structures these models have been proposed in literature. Chapter 6 deals with performance models for tree-based index structures. We analyze models for index structures with the extension of aggregated data in the inner nodes and index structures without the extension. Then we apply three performance models for index structures without aggregated data which are known from literature. We extend the models so that they are applicable to model index structures with aggregated data. Then we introduce a new and better model: PISA (*P*erformance of *I*ndex *S*tructures with and without *A*ggregated data). The PISA model considers the distribution of data and the distribution of queries. Experiments determine the accuracy of models for different data sets. The PISA model is in most scenarios more accurate than the other models. We can decide under which conditions the use of the index structure with aggregated data increases the performance of the index structure to the highest degree.

Chapter 7. For range queries on aggregated data, the R_a^*-tree promises to be an efficient structure. However, tree structures have one major drawback: Tree structures degenerate when the number of dimensions increases as usually this is the case in data warehouse systems. Another class of index structures, the bitmap indexes, try to overcome the problem of degeneration by storing the data of each dimension separately and allowing fast access to those dimensions necessary to answer queries. The question arises which structure is best suited for certain applications. We select and investigate the parameters which influence the performance of the index structures. We apply two techniques to compare different index structures. A first method uses classification trees to visualize rules which are generated from a number of cases. Classification trees show which parameters influence the performance of the index structure more than other parameters. Then a second technique project multidimensional spaces into two dimensions which can be visualized in scatter diagrams. Our results show that by exploiting the evolving disk technology bitmap indexes become more time efficient in comparison to the tree-based index structures.

Chapter 8. The last chapter summarizes the contributions of this thesis. We briefly point out possible further research directions.

2 State of the Art of Data Warehouse Research

We are drowning in data, but starving for knowledge!

(anonymous)

Data warehouse systems are a new technology and differ much from traditional transaction-oriented operational database systems. This chapter describes the major differences between the two concepts and their implications.

2.1 Introduction

Companies have invested much effort during the last decades in the area of information technology. Much of the work was performed to optimize the transaction-oriented systems whose main goal it is to react on customers' orders as fast and as cost-efficiently as possible. Companies have realized that valuable information is stored in their databases. The use of this information can help them to act more efficiently. Operational systems do not support the extraction of information out of databases efficiently because they were not designed for that kind of queries. Even today there is no technology available which supports both kinds of applications. Therefore, new systems are designed and implemented which support the decision making process. These systems are called *data warehouses*. The specific properties of these systems are described in this chapter. The chapter discusses approaches on how to process queries in a data warehouse efficiently.

2.2 Traditional Transaction-Oriented Systems

Most of today's application systems follow a three-layer architecture. The upper level is the presentation layer. Typically *G*raphical *U*ser *I*nterfaces (GUI) visualize the data for the user. The application layer in the middle includes the program logic that covers the application itself, but no data is stored on this level. The data is stored in the third tier, the database layer. Applications change data by invoking operations like insert, update, and delete on the database. A sequence of operations is performed together as a transaction.

These transactions have four properties: *A*tomicity, *C*onsistency, *I*solation, and *D*urability. They are abbreviated as ACID [Härder and Reuter, 1983] . Such applications are called On-Line Transaction Processing (OLTP) applications. Figure 2.1 shows an architecture with two OLTP applications accessing their databases. Graefe gives a general survey on query processing for these kinds of systems [Graefe, 1993].

Once the transaction-oriented data is stored in a database, a Decision Support System (DSS) is often built to create reports by grouping and summarizing data stored in the operational databases. There are various names for these kinds of systems; for instance, reporting tools, Management Information Systems (MIS), or executive information systems [Hannig, 1996]. In contrast to OLTP applications which read/write data from the operational databases, a DSS only reads data to get new information from the data sources. Figure 2.1 shows a DSS at the right side.

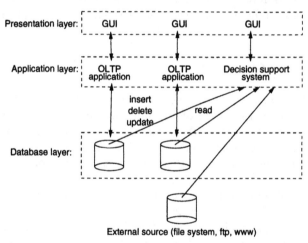

Fig. 2.1. OLTP application and information system based on operational database(s)

A benefit of this approach is that only the operational databases have to be created and maintained. A common set of metadata is used for both the operational system and the added-on DSS. The administration overhead for the DSS is rather small. However, there are significant disadvantages when the DSS and the transaction oriented application software share the same databases. The DSS can only use the actual data that is stored in the operational database. Therefore, historic analysis are usually not possible due to update or delete operations which changed the *historic* data. The operational database is optimized for transaction processes in a multi-user mode. This includes locking operations which do not support a scan of large sets of tuples well. Analytical queries often scan large amounts of tuples. These long transactions significantly decrease the performance of the operational database system. The solution which is usually applied to avoid these problems is to physically separate the transaction-oriented database from the database for the DSS. This information system is called a **data warehouse**.

2.3 Data Warehouses for Decision Support

Inmon defined the term **data warehouse** as a *subject oriented, integrated, time variant, and non-volatile collection of data in support of management's decision making process* [Inmon, 1996]. In detail a data warehouse is:

Subject oriented. The goal of the data in the data warehouse is to improve decision making, planing, and control of the major subjects of enterprises such as customer relations, products, regions in contrast to OLTP applications that are organized around the work-flows of the company.

Integrated. The data in the data warehouse is loaded from different sources that store the data in different formats. The data has to be checked, cleansed and transformed into a unified format to allow easy and fast access.

Time variant. In operational systems, data is valid as of the moment of access, whereas in data warehouse systems the data is valid as of a defined moment of time.

Non-volatile. After the data is inserted in the data warehouse it is neither changed nor removed. The only exceptions are that *false* data is inserted or the capacity of the data warehouse is exceeded and archiving becomes necessary.

Data warehouses are physically separated from the operational DBMS. Such an architecture is shown in Figure 2.2. The data warehouse integrates data from multiple heterogeneous sources to support the need for structured and/or ad-hoc queries, analytical reporting, and decision support. This kind of application is called *On Line Analytical Processing* (OLAP). OLAP allows the transformation of data into strategic information. Codd defined twelve *golden OLAP rules* [Codd, 1994]. Table 2.1 presents the name of these rules. The size of a data warehouse can be in the range of TB (10^{12} Bytes). According to the MetaGroup study *1999 Data Warehouse Marketing Trends/Opportunities* more than 30 % of all data warehouse installations store more than 1 TB, and 14 % of all data warehouse installations have more than 1,000 users.

A data warehouse system DW can formally be defined as a tuple consisting of one target database TDB, *metadata*, and a set OP of operations:

$$DW = (TDB, metadata, OP)$$

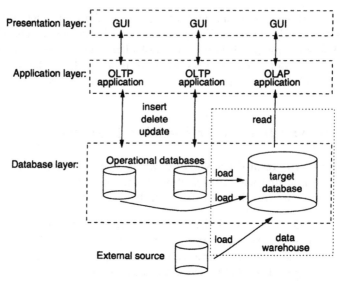

Fig. 2.2. Distinct databases for the transaction-oriented applications and the TDB the for information system/OLAP application

Table 2.1. Twelve golden OLAP rules as defined by Codd

Transparency	Multidimensional conceptual view
Accessibility	Consistent reporting performance
Client-server architecture	Dynamic sparse matrix handling
Generic dimensionality	Unrestricted cross-dimensional operations
Multi-user support	Intuitive data manipulation
Flexible reporting	Unlimited dimensions and aggregation levels

The TDB is the target database for the loaded and transformed data. On this database analytical queries are performed. The set OP of operations is partitioned into four different groups:

Extraction. Extraction operations filter data from different internal or external data sources into temporary data bases. The sources are databases, flat files, web sites etc.

Transformation. These operations transform extracted data into an uniform format. Model-, schema-, and data- conflicts are resolved during the transformation phase.

Load. The load operations load the transformed data into the target database TDB.

Aggregating and grouping. The target database of the data warehouse system does not only store operational data, but also aggregated data. Aggregate and group operations calculate summarized data from base data.

Metadata such as descriptions of data structures stored at different sources, supports each of the above groups of operations. Metadata in the data warehouse system is even more important than in operational systems [Anahory and Murray, 1997]. Metadata is used to check the consistency of data and to ensure that only *safe operations* [Lenz and Shoshani, 1997] are performed.

The target database is usually implemented with a relational DBMS (RDBMS) because this technology is well understood and able to handle large sets of data. However, the index structures investigated in this thesis can be applied to other kinds of DBMSs, too. OLAP applications that are based on RDBMS are also called Relational ROLAP (ROLAP).

2.4 OLAP Vs. OLTP

Once the data is stored in the data warehouse, it is used to create new information for decision making processes. Typical OLAP operations are drill down, roll up, and slice & dice [Inmon, 1996], [Inmon et al., 1997].

Table 2.2. Differences between OLTP and OLAP

aspect	**OLTP**	**OLAP**
level of data	detailed	aggregated
amount of data per transaction	small	large
views	pre-defined	user-defined
typical write operation	update, insert, delete	bulk insert
"age" of data	current (60 - 90 days)	historical, current, predicted, 5 - 10 years
tables	flat tables	multidimensional tables
number of users	high	low-med
data availability	high	low-med
database size	med ($10^9\ B - 10^{12}\ B$)	high ($10^{12}\ B - 10^{15}\ B$)
query optimizing	much experience	new

Table 2.2 summarizes the differences between classical OLTP applications and OLAP applications. In OLTP operations the user changes the database via transactions on detailed data. A typical transaction in a banking environment transfers money from one account to another account. The four ACID properties are essential for this kind of application, because otherwise money

may get lost or get doubled. In OLAP applications the typical user is an analyst who tries to select data needed for decision making. He is primarily not interested in detailed data, but usually in aggregated data over large sets of data. A typical OLAP query is to calculate the average amount of money that customers between age of 20 and 30 withdraw from ATMs in a certain region. For that kind of query the DBMS does not change any data. Hence no locking is necessary. Since the result is calculated by summing up values from many different tuples, fast access to the data has to be supported. The user directs any query in an ad-hoc manner to the system. There exist approaches to model the behavior of the user [Sapia, 1999]. Based on such models the next queries of a user is predicted and pre-computed. This pre-computation decrease the waiting time for the user significantly and the interaction of a user with a data warehouse will become more efficiently.

OLAP and data warehouses are similar to statistical databases that have been discussed for many years [Lenz, 1993], [Lamersdorf et al., 1996], [Shoshani, 1997].

2.5 Accelerating Query Speed

The previous paragraph demonstrates the importance for having fast access to the data stored in the data warehouse. In the typical data warehouse environment, some requirements are less important than in the OLTP applications, e. g. locking and normalization. The overall goal of a data warehouse is to give the user a tool for interactive decision support. This implies that the user needs fast access to large sets of data integrated from different sources. In the remaining part of this chapter, five techniques are discussed that decrease the response time of the system. The speed-up of access to data is achieved if typical requirements of transaction-oriented systems are relaxed. Also redundancy of data increases the storage and update cost, but can reduce the query response time.

2.5.1 Denormalized Schemas

The choice of a data model is essential for any database design. Most OLTP systems are designed on the conceptual level with entity relationship models and then transformed into relational models. The relation schemas are normalized to avoid insert-, update-, or delete-anomalies and redundancy. In data warehouse applications it is more important to have fast access to data than to avoid anomalies. Therefore, the relation schemas are usually not normalized. This implies redundancy in the data and makes manipulative operations more expensive than in databases with normalized schemas.

In a data warehouse multidimensional data is stored. A dimension is defined over a dimensional schema which is a set of functionally interrelated

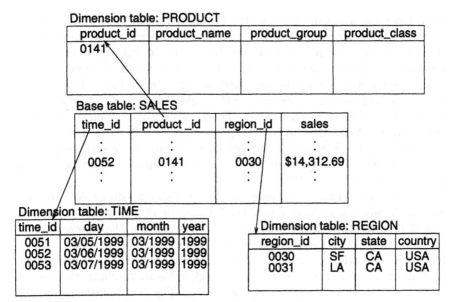

Dimension table: PRODUCT

product_id	product_name	product_group	product_class
0141			

Base table: SALES

time_id	product_id	region_id	sales
:	:	:	:
0052	0141	0030	$14,312.69
:	:	:	:

Dimension table: TIME

time_id	day	month	year
0051	03/05/1999	03/1999	1999
0052	03/06/1999	03/1999	1999
0053	03/07/1999	03/1999	1999

Dimension table: REGION

region_id	city	state	country
0030	SF	CA	USA
0031	LA	CA	USA

Fig. 2.3. Instance of a star schema

dimensional attributes [Lehner et al., 1998]. Dimensional attributes describe categorical attributes and properties like "brand".

The most popular denormalized schema of a data warehouse is the star schema [Chaudhuri and Dayal, 1997]. A star schema consists of one base or fact table in the center surrounded by dimension tables . Figure 2.3 shows an example of a star schema. The denormalization becomes evident in the following examples: the same state belongs always to the same country (e. g. LA and SF belong both to CA and therefore both to the USA). The dependency between CA and USA is stored several times in the relation **region**. There are other dependencies in the relation **time** between **month** and the **year**.

Other schemas used for data warehouses include galaxy schema and snowflake schema [Anahory and Murray, 1997]. A set of base tables with some mutual dimension tables is called a galaxy schema. A star schema with normalized dimension tables is called a snowflake schema.

2.5.2 Materialized Views

One widely used strategy of accelerating the access to aggregated data is to pre-compute *materialized views* [Gupta et al., 1997]. Base tables of a data warehouse may contain several millions of tuples. Therefore, scanning these base relations can take a significant amount of time. If there is some knowledge on what kind of queries the analysts will ask, these queries are pre-computed and the results are stored in materialized views. The access to pre-computed data is much faster than computing data on demand. However, the main technical problems are that the pre-computation takes time, the pre-computed data needs space, and it is difficult to predict what kind of data the user is interested in. There are additional semantical problems, *e. g.* the integrity constraints have to be satisfied. The data for pre-computation has to be selected along three criteria. First, an aggregation function (*e. g.* sum, max, min, avg, median, mostFrequent) is selected. Second, the dimensions are chosen; the data is aggregated with the group-by-statement. Third, in case of hierarchical attributes, the aggregation level is fixed. Data that is stored on a daily base can be summarized to data for weeks, months, or years. The size of the different views can be estimated without calculating the views [Shukla et al., 1996].

Assume three-dimensional sales data exist with time dimension, product dimension, and region dimension RSALES(<u>time</u>, <u>product</u>, <u>region</u>, sales). The three attributes time, product, and region are the categorical attributes. They define the three dimensions of the data. The attribute sales is the summary attribute and holds the information about the sales in a certain time about a certain product in a certain region. Figure 2.4 shows the base relation with all three dimensions at the bottom. The base relation is denoted by (t, p, r). From this base relation various marginal relations (subcubes) are computed by summarizing the data. For example RSALESpr(<u>product</u>, <u>region</u> ,sales) is computed by the following SQL statement:

```
CREATE VIEW RSALESpr AS
SELECT product,region,SUM(sales)
FROM RSALES
GROUP BY product,region
```

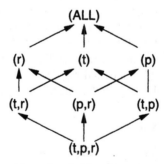

Fig. 2.4. Lattice of base table and subcubes/margins

In general, the base data is stored in a fact table $R(a_1, \cdots, a_n, s)$. The variables a_1 to a_n denote the categorical attributes and s is the summary attribute. Figure 2.4 presents the whole lattice of relations. An arrow from (p, t, r) to (p, r) denotes the fact that (p, r) is computable from (p, t, r). (p, t, r) can be seen as a three-dimensional data cube and (p, r) as one of its two-dimensional subcubes. (ALL) denotes the aggregate over all values. In general a n-dimensional data cube (without any hierarchical attributes) has $\binom{n}{k}$ k-dimensional subcubes. Therefore, a n-dimensional data cube has $\sum_{k=0}^{n} \binom{n}{k} = 2^n$ subcubes. If hierarchical attributes are considered, the number of possible subcubes is even bigger. The (automatic) selection of views that should be materialized is an actual research topic and known as the *view selection problem* [Gupta et al., 1997]. There are several different ways to choose the views for materialization such as Exhaustive search, Greedy algorithms [Gupta et al., 1997], A*-Algorithm [Labio et al., 1997], Integer programming [Yang et al., 1997], and Genetic algorithms [Lee and Hammer, 1999].

None of the five approaches has proven to be dominant. Once the views are selected and are materialized, another problem arises. Each time a base table is changed, the materialized views and indexes built on it have to be updated (or at least have to be checked whether some changes have to be propagated or not). The views and the indexes can be updated incrementally or from the scratch. The problem of updating the views is known as the *view maintenance problem* [Huyn, 1997].

2.5.3 No Locking

Since analysts only read data of a data warehouse and do not change tuples, a locking mechanism is not necessary. Data is changed only when it is inserted from external data sources. This is scheduled for example at night when no analyst is allowed to access the data. Overhead is decreased and query processing accelerated if no locking mechanism is applied.

2.5.4 On-line Aggregation

The execution of typical OLAP queries can take much time and the user waits for the final answer until the query is processed completely. There are applications where the user is more interested in having an approximate result after a short time than getting a very precise answer after a long time period. One approach is the use of on-line aggregation where the user is informed about the actual status of his query during query processing [Hellerstein et al., 1997a], [Haas, 1999]. He can stop the execution of the query at any time and gets the result that is computed so far. This possibility of interactive query control significantly reduces the work load of the database server. However, some techniques have to be applied to guarantee that the data is processed in the system in random order.

2.5.5 Index Structures

During the last three decades a great deal of research has been performed in the area of index structures for DBMSs. Starting with the B-tree [Bayer and McCreight, 1972] many new structures have been developed [Gaede and Günther, 1998]. The B-tree is an optimal structure for dynamic indexing of one-dimensional data for many applications. Almost all DBMSs implement the B-tree. No tree structure has been published that has the same properties for the multidimensional case as the B-tree in one dimension.

Due to the large sets of multidimensional data that are stored in data warehouse systems, table scans should be avoided whenever possible by the use of index structures. Because the kind of data and the typical queries that are processed in data warehouse systems differ much from traditional transaction-oriented applications, evaluation is important which index structures are suited best for these applications.

This thesis focuses on finding index structures that index typical data warehouse data efficiently. Chapter 5 describes an extension to improve multidimensional tree structures which perform significantly faster for range queries on aggregated data. Performance models are developed to show how this extension influences the performance of tree structures. Chapter 6 investigates these performance models in detail. DBMSs that are designed for data warehousing have implemented bitmap indexing techniques besides the classic index structures. (e. g. [Sybase, 1997]). The bitmap indexing techniques are promising techniques for indexing typical data warehouse data and processing data warehouse queries efficiently. Chapter 7 describes and applies techniques for comparing different index structures. We present results of the comparative study.

2.6 Summary

This chapter described the major research topics in data warehousing. We defined the term *data warehouse* and investigated the differences between OLAP and OLTP applications. The main task in data warehousing is to provide the analyst with a tool for having fast access to aggregates over large sets of data that are integrated from different sources. Usually, this data is stored in a relational DBMS. The facts are stored in a fact table like $R(\underline{time, product, region}, sales)$. In general, the data is stored in a fact table $R(a_1, \cdots, a_n, s)$. One of the main goals of a data warehouse system is to decrease the query response time as much as possible. Five different mechanisms were described to speed up queries. The main part of the thesis focuses on what kind of index structures are used to speed up queries in data warehouse systems and how the behavior of such structures can be estimated and compared.

3 Data Storage and Index Structures

640 K ought to be enough for anybody.   Bill Gates

One important property of DBMSs is their ability to handle large amounts of data. In order to store and retrieve this data efficiently different techiques are applied. This chapter introduces basic methods that are relevant to save and search large sets of data as they are typical in data warehouse systems.

3.1 Introduction

Data warehouses store huge sets of multidimensional data. The databases of such a system can be as large as TB of data. Data of this size does not fit into main memory and is therefore stored on secondary or even on tertiary memory. To process the data and use it for computations within the CPU the data is transfered through different components of a computer system. These components are reviewed in a memory hierarchy. We describe the memory hierarchy that is typical for today's computer systems. Fast accesses to the data stored on secondary memory have to be provided to retrieve the data. The mechanics of the disks influence the performance of the index structures and is therefore investigated here.

We map the multidimensional tuples stored in the data warehouse into a multidimensional data space. We define the data space and the typical queries processed on the data. In order to process the specified queries efficiently different access structures have been designed in academic research. We present different kinds of structures and concentrate on tree-based based index structures and bitmap indexes.

3.2 Memory Hierarchy

The major characteristic of such computer systems which the DBMSs run on is the memory hierarchy consisting of five levels [Gray and Reuter, 1993], [Härder and Rahm, 1999], [Garcia-Molina et al., 1999], [Saake and Heuer, 1999].

M. Juergens: Index Structures for Data Warehouses, LNCS 1859, pp. 15-34, 2002.
© Springer-Verlag Berlin Heidelberg 2002

CPU registers are the fastest storage devices of a computer system and store the operands of computations. The next level is the cache. For read operations each value in a cache is a copy of some value in the main memory. There are often two kinds of cache. One small cache is integrated on the processor chip. One other larger second level cache is placed on a separate chip. The main memory is a volatile storage and ranges from 128 MB to more than 10 GB for typical machines. Main memory is accessed randomly and access time ranges between 10^{-8} and 10^{-7} seconds.

The secondary memory is a non-volatile storage. The random access to disk is usually more than 10^5 times slower than the access to main memory. In database systems, transfering the data from the disk into main memory is the main performance bottleneck. The cost models in this thesis are based on the accesses to disks.

Tertiary memory has larger capabilities than secondary memory, but slower access times. Typical kinds of tertiary storage systems are: ad-hoc tape storages, optical-disk juke boxes, and tape silos. Tertiary storage access is approximately 1,000 times slower than secondary memory access but can be 1,000 times more capacious. In data warehouse environments it often archives and backups data.

3.3 Mechanics of Disks

The complete database of a data warehouse does not usually fit into the main memory of a computer system. Therefore, the database is stored on the next level of the memory hierarchy, the secondary memory. As previously mentioned, access to secondary memory is more than 100,000 times slower than access to main memory. Often, this access to secondary memory is the bottleneck of a DBMS.

However, not all accesses to secondary memory are equal. Reading blocks sequentially from hard disks is much faster than random access.

A disk consists of a number of platters rotating around a central spindle. Each platter has two surfaces that are covered with magnetic material. Figure 3.1 sketches a disk with three platters and six surfaces. The bits are stored sequentially in concentric circles on the surfaces that are called tracks. Each track consists of a fixed number of sectors.

When data is requested from the disk complete sectors of data are read. Physical sectors are mapped to logical blocks. Often the terms "pages" or "chunks" are used in the same context. In this thesis we assume that one block is mapped to a fixed number of sectors and we use the words block and sectors interchangeable. The size of a block in KB is denoted by blocksize b.

As previously mentioned, the access to a block on secondary memory can be performed in two different modes. The time t_s for a sequential block access (transfer_time) is calculated by [Härder and Rahm, 1999]:

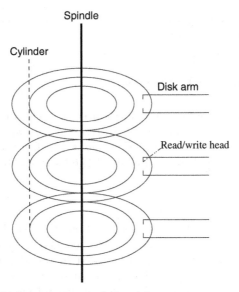

Fig. 3.1. Disk with three platters and six surfaces

$$t_s = \text{transfer\_time} = \frac{b * 1024}{\text{transfer\_rate}} \tag{3.1}$$

The time t_r for a random block access is calculated by:

$$t_r = \text{seek\_time} + \frac{\text{rotation\_time}}{2} + \text{transfer\_time} \tag{3.2}$$

With today's hard drives and block sizes of 4 KB the time t_r for a random block access is approximately 10 to 20 times larger than t_s. This difference in access time increases the performance of structures which access large contiguous portions of data at the same time.

Experimental studies show that the seek_time and the rotation_time decrease by only 8 % per year, while the transfer_rate increases by 40 % per year [Patterson and Keeton, 1998], [Bitton and Gray, 1998]. Therefore, the ratio between the time for a random block access t_r and the time for a sequential block access t_s increases significantly. Sequential disk accesses are getting disproportionately cheaper. This difference between the sequential and random access times implies two facts that become even more important in the future:

1. If more than a certain fraction (approximately 5 to 10 %) of the data has to be accessed, a full table scan is faster than the use of a tree-based index structure. This fraction is decreasing every year.
2. For a comparison of different access structures it is not sufficient to count only the block I/Os . The number of random block accesses and sequential block accesses have to be weighted differently.

In the next chapters we will consider these two facts and use them for the comparison of index structures.

3.4 Data Space and Queries

We assume the data of a fact table introduced in Section has to be indexed. The fact table is the relation schema $R(a_1, a_2, \cdots, a_n, s)$, where a_j are the key attributes and the names of the *dimensions*. The fact attribute is denoted as s. Each dimension a_j has the domain A_j and s is a summary value.

3.4.1 Data Space

Without loss of generality we assume that an index is built on the first $d \in \{1, \cdots, n\}$ attributes. The index structure does not consider the other $(n - d)$ attributes. Pointers (*tid*) are stored in the leaf nodes of the index structure to point to the locations where the complete tuples are stored [Härder and Rahm, 1999]. We assume that all indexed attributes are discrete values. The cardinality of the different domains A_j is given by $c_j = |A_j|$ for all $j \in \{1, \cdots, d\}$. Each set A_j is coded to a set of non-negative integers $O_j = \{0, \cdots, c_j - 1\}$.

Definition 3.4.1. *The d-dimensional data space is defined as the set* $O = O_1 \times \cdots \times O_d$.

For each tuple of relation R one index entry (p, tid) is created, where $p \in O$ and $tid \in TID$ is a unique Tuple IDentifier and TID is the set of all correct Tuple IDentifiers. The set of all index entries is $A \subset O \times TID$ where $\forall (p_1, tid_1), (p_2, tid_2) \in A : tid_1 = tid_2 \Rightarrow p_1 = p_2$.

For storing set A, this set is partitioned into subsets which store the elements of each subset on one block. When partitioning A into subsets the tuples, that have points which are close to each other, should be in the same block. Each block is represented often by a minimum bounding box or minimum bounding rectangle that all tuples include. These regions are represented as d-dimensional hyper-rectangles. Definition 3.4.2 specifies these d-dimensional hyper-rectangles.

Definition 3.4.2. *A d-dimensional hyper-rectangle I of the data space O is defined as $I = [l_1, u_1] \times \cdots \times [l_d, u_d] \subset O$ where $l_j \in \{0, \cdots, c_j - 1\}$ is the lower limit in the jth dimension and $u_j \in \{0, \cdots, c_j - 1\}$ is the upper limit in the jth dimension $(l_j \leq u_j) \forall j \in \{1, \cdots, d\}$.*

3.4.2 Queries

An index structure processes different kinds of queries. We define the most important query types below.

Point queries. Point queries retrieve all elements of a specific point p.

Definition 3.4.3. *A point query $PQ : O \rightarrow 2^A$ with $PQ(p) = \{(p, tid) \in A\}$ is a query that returns all elements having exactly the value of point p.*

Range queries. Range queries retrieve all elements that are contained in a d-dimensional hyper-rectangle I.

Definition 3.4.4. *A range query $RQ : 2^I \rightarrow 2^A$ with $RQ(I) = \{(p, tid) \in A | p \in I\}$ is a query returning all elements where p is included in the range of the hyper-rectangle I.*

The size of a query box is given as $q = (q_1, \cdots, q_d) := (u_1 - l_1, \cdots, u_d - l_d)$. A partial range query is a query with a query box where some dimensions are not restricted. Each partial range query can be simulated by a range query. For each dimension i, for which the partial range query is not restricted, the hyper-rectangle of the range query is set to $l_j = 0$ and $u_j = c_j - 1$. Therefore, we shall only use the term range queries in this thesis.

Nearest neighbor. Nearest neighbor queries are important for similarity search and they retrieve the closest data items to some specified point p.

Definition 3.4.5. *A nearest neighbor query is $NNQ : O \rightarrow 2^A$, where $NNQ(p) = \{p' | \forall p'' : dist(p, p') \leq dist(p, p'')\}$*

The distance between two points is calculated by a function $dist$. Different metrics can be used here, such as Euclidean metric, Manhattan metric, or maximum metric.

The previous definitions characterize the data that is indexed and the queries that are executed. In the context of data warehouses range queries on aggregated data are of main interest. Therefore, we investigate what kind of index structures efficiently support these queries for a given set of data by using the hardware described in Section 3.2 and Section 3.3.

3.5 Tree-Based Indexing

In the beginning there was the B-tree. The B-tree [Bayer and McCreight, 1972] is a widely used one-dimensional tree-based index structure in DBMSs. It is proven that there is no better one-dimensional index structure with the same generality and flexibility than the B-tree. However, there is no general solution on how to apply the B-tree for indexing multidimensional data.

One method is to generate one B-tree for each attribute. If there is a range query in more than one dimension, the B-trees for all selected dimensions are applied. If $d = 2$, the result sets r_1 and r_2 of the indexes are calculated and intersected. The left side of Figure 3.2 shows this approach. The result sets

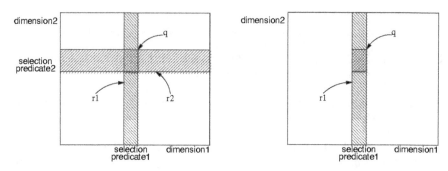

Two B-trees: Result sets r_1 and r_2 One B-tree: Result set r_1 has to be
have to be intersected   evaluated completely

Fig. 3.2. Use of B-tree for multidimensional data $(d = 2)$

of $predicate_1$ and $predicate_2$ of query q is calculated by selecting all tuples
that are in both result sets.

Another possibility is the use of just one B-tree. For example, the B-tree
in dimension 1 is used. Then each tuple that belongs to the result set r_1 is
loaded and we evaluate if the tuple satisfies $predicate_2$. This idea is sketched
on the right side of Figure 3.2. However, this approach has the main drawback
that much more tuples are loaded and evaluated than actually belong to the
result set.

A third alternative to index multidimensional data with one-dimensional
B-trees uses compound indexes. For each permutation of a set of dimensions
a one-dimensional index is built. In our example the indexes a_1, a_2 and index
a_2, a_1 are created. The number of necessary indexes is the main disadvantage
of this approach. For d-dimensional data $d!$ indexes must be created and must
be maintained. This approach is not feasible for high dimensional data.

A fourth option is the mapping of the multidimensional data space
into a one-dimensional data space with a space filling function. A space
filling function defines a one-dimensional ordering for a multidimensional
space [Markl, 1999], see Section 3.5.7.

The remainder of this chapter discusses some basic properties of multidimensional index structures. We cannot give a complete survey; we rather
simply sketch some ideas that help us to understand what index structures for
secondary memory are used in the context of indexing data warehouse data
efficiently. For further details we refer to standard references [Samet, 1989],
[Samet, 1990], [Gaede and Günther, 1998].

3.5.1 Top-Down, Bottom-Up, and Bulk Loading

For a given set of data there are two approaches in creating index structures.
The first approach is the top-down method; that is the data is added from the

root to the leafs in the tree. The top-down approach should only be applied, if all of the data is not known in advance and data has to be inserted and deleted frequently. The second approach is the bottom-up method. Here, the leafs are created first. Then the upper levels of the tree are built successively from the bottom to the top. The bottom-up approach works best, if all data is known in advance and no changes are made after the create phase. Hybrid techniques can be applied. In this case the index is created efficiently with a bottom-up technique and changes are propagated with the top-down method.

Inserting data in a multidimensional index structure incrementally is expensive. An approach to alleviate this problem is to attach a buffer to each node [van den Bercken et al., 1997]. If the node exceeds its capacity tuples are loaded into the buffer. This allows inserting many tuples at the same time and postponing the expensive split operations. Related techniques are the small-tree-large-tree approach [Chen et al., 1998] and the buffer tree [Arge, 1995].

3.5.2 Point Quadtrees

Point quadtrees [Finkel and Bentley, 1974] are multidimensional extensions of binary trees. Two-dimensional point quadtrees ($d = 2$) divide the data space into non uniformly sized cells. Each cell stores up to a fixed number of data points. Once the capacity is exceeded, the cell is split into the $2^d = 4$ sub-cells: NE, SE, SW, and NW clockwise in this order. The left side of Figure 3.3 represents some cells in a plane while the right side of the same figure shows the structure of the quadtree.

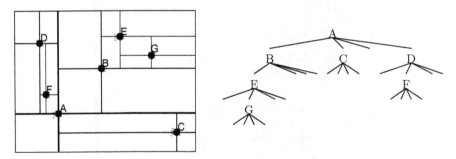

Fig. 3.3. Point quadtree: Data space and tree representation

The main drawback of this structure is that each node that exceeds its capacity is split into four sub-nodes in the two-dimensional case. Therefore, the minimal number of entries per node can be as low as $\frac{1}{4}$ of the maximum capacity. For the three-dimensional case this structure is also called octree. If a split occurs in the octree, each node is split into eight sub-nodes. In general, for a d-dimensional tree each split creates 2^d descendants. Therefore, the average space utilization might be low for a high number of dimensions.

3.5.3 kd-tree

The kd-tree [Bentley, 1975] is in contrast to the point quadtree a binary tree. A node split in a kd-tree is processed by splitting a node into two child nodes according to one dimension. The dimension for that the split is chosen either randomly or according to some rules. The kd-tree guarantees that each leaf nodes is filled by at least 50 %. However, the top down approach of the kd-tree is an unbalanced index structure.

3.5.4 kdb-tree

The **kdb**-tree [Robinson, 1981] combines the balanced structure of the B-tree and the multidimensional features of the kd-tree. The path from the root to the leafs has always the same length; some pages may be split without any overflow. This effect is called *cascade splitting* and might generate some nodes without any entries. Figure 3.4 shows a kdb-tree in which coordinates of cities in California are inserted. In the lower left corner *cascade splits* generate empty pages.

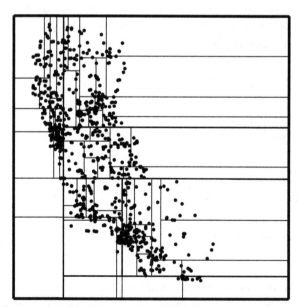

Fig. 3.4. kdb-tree with 1,000 locations in California

3.5.5 R-tree

The R-tree [Guttman, 1984] is a multidimensional generalization of the B-tree. In contrast to the B-tree which uses one-dimensional intervals as atomar elements, the R-tree applies multidimensional rectangles to represent multidimensional intervals. The R-tree consists of two different types of nodes. *Leaf* nodes and *non-leaf* nodes. *Leaf* nodes contain entries of the form $(tid, rectangle)$ with tids referring to records in the database. *Non-leaf* nodes contain entries of the form $(cp, rectangle)$ with cp being a pointer to a child node of the R-tree and *rectangle* being the minimum bounding rectangle of all rectangles which are entries of that child node (cf. Figure 3.5). Each rectangle is represented as a hyper-rectangle respectively a hyper-interval I as defined in Definition 3.4.2 on page 18. *Non-leaf* nodes are used to direct the path to the *leaf* nodes. Therefore, they are also called directory nodes.

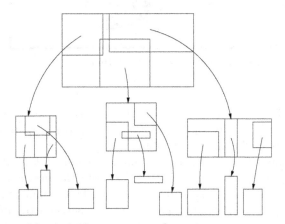

Fig. 3.5. R-tree with rectangles as atomar elements

In contrast to the B-tree and the other index structures, the R-tree contains overlaps of regions. This implies, that no worst case analysis is possible. For a point query there can be ambiguous ways that have to be traversed. The R^+-tree [Sellis et al., 1985] is an approach to overcome this problem by using clipping to prevent overlaps. There are several other extension of the R-tree, some of which are briefly discussed in the next two sections.

3.5.6 R*-tree

The R^*-tree [Beckmann et al., 1990] provides a better insertion algorithm than the R-tree. It uses a *forced reinsert* mechanism to reorganize the structure. This mechanism enables the structure to adapt to data distributions

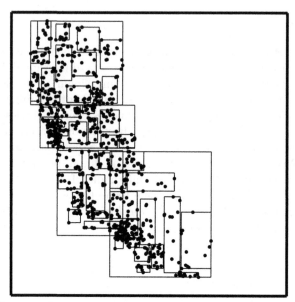

Fig. 3.6. R^*-tree with 1,000 locations in California

and not to suffer from rectangles inserted previously. Experimental comparisons of the R-tree family show that the R^*-tree performs faster than the other structures [Beckmann et al., 1990].

The maximum fanout B and the minimum fanout b of the nodes are important parameters for trees. Let B_{dir} denote the maximum number of directory entries fitting in one node and let b_{dir} be the minimum number of entries in a directory node. The parameter b_{dir} satisfies the following condition: $2 \leq b_{dir} \leq \frac{B_{dir}}{2}$. The parameters B_{leaf} and b_{leaf} are defined in the same way. The ratio between b_{leaf} and B_{leaf} respective b_{dir} and B_{dir} influences the performance of the R^*-tree. A high value of b_{leaf} yields to less leaf nodes, but to more overlaps between the regions of different nodes on the same level. Beckmann *et al.* got the best tradeoff for $\frac{b_{dir}}{B_{dir}} = \frac{b_{leaf}}{B_{leaf}} = 0.4$ [Beckmann et al., 1990]. In experiments later presented in this thesis this value is used as well.

3.5.7 Other Relatives of the R-tree Family and Other Tree Structures

There are many different extensions besides the R^+-tree and the R^*-tree to improve the performance of the R-tree. This section discusses some approaches briefly.

The packed-R-tree [Roussopoulos and Leifker, 1985] is a bottom-up structure and clusters data items together in a data node according to a nearest

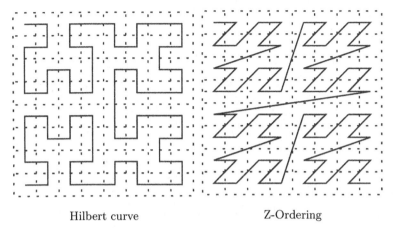

Hilbert curve   Z-Ordering

Fig. 3.7. Space filling curves

neighbor function. The idea of the Hilbert R-tree [Kamel and Faloutsos, 1994] is to cluster the data together in nodes of the same level according to a Hilbert curve (cf. left part of Figure 3.7). The Hilbert curve is applied to calculate a one-dimensional Hilbert value for multidimensional points/rectangles. The points are then clustered according to their Hilbert values. The rectangles are clustered according to the Hilbert value of their center. The HG-tree [Kuan and Lewis, 1999] is a multidimensional tree structure designed for point data based on the Hilbert R-tree. The Simple Tile R-tree (STR-tree) [Leutenegger et al., 1997] is a bottom-up structure like the packed R-tree, but it applies the Sort-Tile-Recursive algorithm to cluster rectangles. The X-tree [Berchtold et al., 1996] is an R^*-tree with variable size of nodes. The size of a node can be enlarged to prevent node splitting that would yield to nodes with large overlaps.

Rectangles are not well suited for nearest neighbor queries. The SS-tree [White and Jain, 1996] uses spheres instead of rectangles. Figure 3.8 shows an example to organize the data. A benefit of this structure is that a region is defined by storing one d-dimensional point and the radius. Only $(d + 1)$ numbers are stored for each region, whereas the R-tree defines its regions with $2d$ coordinates. The SR-tree [Karayama and Satoh, 1997] is a combination of the SS-tree and R-tree. Weighted dimensions [Großer, 1997] apply a priority scheme to split an R^*-tree more often in selected dimensions than in other dimensions. It is advantageous to split in these dimensions more frequently in which the query boxes are restricted mostly. Another way of improving the performance is achieved by executing R-trees in parallel [Schnitzer and Leutenegger, 1999].

A flexible tree structure for indexing spatial objects is the cell tree [Günther, 1989]. Figure 3.9 shows an example of the cell tree. The cell

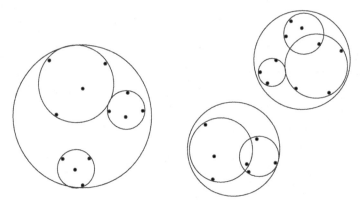

Fig. 3.8. SS-tree width spheres as atomar elements

tree does not use hyper-rectangles as atomar data items, but more general polygons.

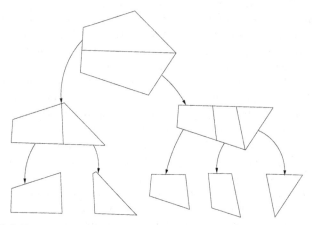

Fig. 3.9. Cell Tree with polygons as atomar elements

The idea of the UB-tree [Bayer, 1996], [Bayer and Markl, 1998], [Markl, 1999] is to sort the multidimensional data according to the Z-ordering (cf. right part of Figure 3.7). For each multidimensional point the corresponding Z-value of the square in which the point is contained is calculated. The corresponding Z-values are then indexed using a B-tree.

3.5.8 Generic Tree Structures

During the last years many different index structures have been developed. Some of them are presented in this chapter. New index structures differ often just in a few details from existing ones. Therefore, some approaches are developed to provide generic frameworks where the common part of the index structures is given by the system and only the differences are specified and implemented by researcher and developer. One approach is the *Generalized Search Tree* (GiST) [Hellerstein et al., 1995], [Kornacker et al., 1997], [Kornacker, 1999] where different index structures are implemented by just defining the four functions *consistent, union, penalty,* and *picksplit.* The *Access Method DeBuging tool* (AMDB) [Kornacker et al., 1998] illustrates for a given data and query set the performance of the structure. Gurret et al. focuses mainly on spatial benchmarks [Gurret and Rigaux, 1998] and implement different spatial index structures and join algorithms in one framework. The performance therefore can be compared easily. Günther et al. discuss related techniques for comparing spatial join algorithms [Günther et al., 1998].

3.6 Bitmap Indexing

Bitmap indexing is rather different from the tree-based indexing considered previously. One of the main benefit of bitmap indexing techniques is that they are easy to implement. In addition, the operations of the bitmap indexing techniques are mostly reading large blocks of bits and Boolean operations on vectors of bits (bitmap vectors). These operations are performed very efficiently. This is one reason, why bitmap indexing techniques are implemented in commercial database systems, *e. g.* Oracle [Christiansen et al., 1998], Sybase [Sybase, 1997], and Informix [Informix, 1997]. Among the disadvantages of bitmap indexing techniques are the facts that they can be very space consuming and that the insert / update operations are more expensive than for tree-based structures.

O'Neil et al. compare different indexing techniques in a rather qualitative approach [O'Neil and Quass, 1997]. Equality encoded and range encoded indexing techniques [Chan and Ioannidis, 1998] are promising structures for *read-mostly* environments. Interval encoded bitmap indexing techniques [Chan and Ioannidis, 1999] are optimal under certain conditions. In the presence of hierarchies of the attributes special bitmap structures are used by some bitmap indexing techniques [Wu and Buchmann, 1998].

3.6.1 Standard Bitmap Indexing

The idea of bitmap indexing is simple. First, we treat each dimension separately. For each attribute a_j a number of c_j bitmap vectors are generated, with $c_j = |A_j|$. Each bitmap vector has a length of t bits, where t is the

$\pi_{a_1}(R)$	B^{11}	B^{10}	B^9	B^8	B^7	B^6	B^5	B^4	B^3	B^2	B^1	B^0
5	0	0	0	0	0	0	1	0	0	0	0	0
3	0	0	0	0	0	0	0	0	1	0	0	0
0	0	0	0	0	0	0	0	0	0	0	0	1
3	0	0	0	0	0	0	0	0	1	0	0	0
11	1	0	0	0	0	0	0	0	0	0	0	0
$\vdots$	$\vdots$	$\vdots$	$\vdots$	$\vdots$	$\vdots$	$\vdots$	$\vdots$	$\vdots$	$\vdots$	$\vdots$	$\vdots$	$\vdots$

Fig. 3.10. Original data and standard bitmap index

number of tuples it indexes. The jth bit of the kth bitmap vector is set to
1, if the jth tuple corresponds to the kth value and it is set to 0 otherwise.
The left side of Figure 3.10 shows the first five rows of the projection of a relation R on attribute a_1. We assume A_1 consists of 12 different values which
are mapped to integer numbers between 0 and 11. Figure 3.10 presents the
bitmap index for this data. Each column B_{11} to B_0 represents one bitmap
vector. If all tuples have to be selected where $a_1 = 3$ the bitmap vector B^3
is read and all tuples, with the bits set to 1, are chosen ($PQ(3) \approx B^3$). Such
a set of bitmap vectors is generated for all dimensions.

If preconditions like $(a_1 = 3) \wedge (a_2 = 2)$ are evaluated, one bitmap vector
for attribute a_1 and one bitmap vector for attribute a_2 are read and a Boolean
AND operation is performed.

The size of the bitmap index depends on the number of tuples and on the
cardinality of the attributes. The size of one bitmap vector given in blocks
is calculated as $v = \lceil \frac{t}{8192*b} \rceil$, where b is the block size in KB and t is the
number of tuples that are indexed. For each element of the domain A_j one
bitmap vector is created. The total number of bitmap vectors is calculated
by:

$$Space = \sum_{i=1}^{d} c_j \tag{3.3}$$

However, bitmap indexes in the form presented here, have some drawbacks.
Firstly, the cardinality of the domain of each attribute has to be known in
advance. In *read-mostly* environments which are in the focus of this thesis
this is a reasonable assumption. A second drawback is, if the cardinality of
the domain is large, standard bitmap indexes become very space consuming.

Finally, range queries are very typical for data warehouse systems. Standard bitmaps are not very efficient for range queries. Consider the above
example from Figure 3.10 and a range query like $2 \leq a_1 \leq 7$. For this query
six bitmap vectors B^2 to B^7 are read and distributively combined as:

$$RQ([2,7]) \approx (B^7 \vee B^6 \vee B^5 \vee B^4 \vee B^3 \vee B^2) \tag{3.4}$$

Alternatively, the bitmaps B^0, B^1 and B^8 to B^{11} are read, distributively
combined and the compliment calculated: $RQ([2,7]) \approx \neg(B^{11} \vee B^{10} \vee B^9 \vee
B^8 \vee B^1 \vee B^0)$. In each case six bitmaps vectors are read.

The next sections describe extensions of bitmap indexing techniques to overcome the above mentioned problems. One approach of multi-component equality encoded bitmap indexes which increases the space efficiency of standard bitmaps is presented. A further approach investigates range encoded bitmap indexes to support range queries more efficiently. A hybrid approach combines both approaches to a space and time efficient index for processing range queries.

3.6.2 Multi-component Equality Encoded Bitmap Index

The equality encoded bitmap index [Chan and Ioannidis, 1998], overcomes the problem of being very space consuming for attributes with large domains. It could be argued, that space is no longer an issue. However, the occupied space is proportional to the time for creating such an index. Therefore, the space measures the creation time and even in *read-mostly* environments this time cannot be neglected. The main idea of compressing bitmap indexes presented here can be seen as an encoding of the values of a_1 into a different number system. For example, the values 0 to 11 from the above example are encoded into the <3,4> number system. Each value $x \in \{0, \cdots, 11\}$ is encoded by $x = (4 * y + z)$ where $y \in \{0, 1, 2\}$ and $z \in \{0, 1, 2, 3\}$, $y :=$ $\lfloor x \div 4 \rfloor$, $z := (x \mod 4)$. The values of y and z are then stored like standard bitmap indexes. Figure 3.11 shows the resulting structure. The main benefit of this approach is the reduced space consumption in comparison with the standard bitmap index. The standard bitmap index in Figure 3.10 needs 12 bitmap vectors. The <3,4> encoded bitmap vector in Figure 3.11 stores seven bitmap vectors. However, the savings in space reduce the time efficiency of the structure. For a point query, two bitmap vectors are read with the <3,4> equality encoded bitmap index. To compute the result for the query $a_1 = 3$ the term $PQ[3] \approx (B_1^0 \wedge B_0^3)$ is evaluated.

$\pi_{a_1}(R)$	B_1^2	B_1^1	B_1^0	B_0^3	B_0^2	B_0^1	B_0^0
5	0	1	0	0	0	1	0
3	0	0	1	1	0	0	0
0	0	0	1	0	0	0	1
3	0	0	1	1	0	0	0
11	1	0	0	1	0	0	0
$\vdots$	$\vdots$	$\vdots$	$\vdots$	$\vdots$	$\vdots$	$\vdots$	$\vdots$
x		y			z		

Fig. 3.11. Base-<3,4> equality encoded bitmap index

For larger attribute cardinality c_j the differences in space and time are even more significant. Consider an example, where $c_1 = 1,000$ different values are indexed. The standard bitmap index can be seen as a <1000>

encoded structure and 1,000 bitmap vectors are created. For each of the values between 0 and 999 one bitmap vector is stored. One way of compression is to decode each digit of the values separately. This $<10,10,10>$ multi-component equality encoded bitmap index stores only 30 bitmap vectors. The number of bitmap vectors, read for a query like $a_i = 352$ is increased from one bitmap vector of term (B^{352}) to three bitmap vectors in term $PQ[352] \approx (B_2^3 \wedge B_1^5 \wedge B_0^2)$, while the number of necessary vectors is decreased.

This example shows the time-space tradeoff. There are four interesting points of this tradeoff: time optimal, space optimal, "knee", and time optimal under given space constraint [Chan and Ioannidis, 1998]. In this example the time optimal index has the base of $<1000>$. This is the standard bitmap index. The space optimal index has the base of $<2,2,2,2,2,2,2,2,2,2>$. This is the binary representation of the values. The more interesting tradeoffs are somewhere in between (e. g. $<34,33>$ or $<10,10,10>$). In the following chapters we construct index structure which are time optimal under given space constraint.

The processing of range queries with a multi-component equality encoded bitmap index is more complex. The query $2 \leq a_1 \leq 7$ is processed by evaluating the expression:

$$RQ([2,7]) \approx \underbrace{(\neg B_1^0 \vee (B_1^0 \wedge (B_0^2 \vee B_0^3)))}_{2 \leq a_1} \wedge \underbrace{\neg B_1^2}_{a_1 \leq 7} \qquad (3.5)$$

Figure 3.12 sketches the algorithm to calculate the base for an equality encoded bitmap index. This algorithm performs for each $j \in \{1, \cdots, d\}$ with the input parameters cardinality of the attribute c_j and the maximum number of bitmap vectors m_j. The output are the number of components n_j and the size of each component (depends on b_j and r_j). An additional optimization step (not shown here), improves the performance of the bitmap index structures [Chan and Ioannidis, 1998]. The base in each dimension j is then given by:

$$< \underbrace{b_j - 1, \cdots, b_j - 1}_{n_j - r_j}, \underbrace{b_j, \cdots, b_j}_{r_j} > \qquad (3.6)$$

In this thesis, the base in the jth dimension is denoted as:

$$< b_{j1}, b_{j2}, \cdots, b_{jn_j} > = < \underbrace{b_j - 1, \cdots, b_j - 1}_{n_j - r_j}, \underbrace{b_j, \cdots, b_j}_{r_j} > \qquad (3.7)$$

For example: b_{23} denotes the base of the third component of the second attribute / dimension. The number of bitmap vectors in all dimensions is:

$$Space = \sum_{j=1}^{d} m_j = \sum_{j=1}^{d} \sum_{i=1}^{r_j} b_{ji} = \sum_{j=1}^{d} ((n_j - r_j)(b_j - 1) + r_j b_j) \qquad (3.8)$$

$$
\begin{array}{l}
n_j = 0 \\
\texttt{repeat} \\
\qquad n_j = n_j + 1 \\
\qquad b_j = \lfloor m_j/n_j \rfloor + 1 \\
\qquad r_j = (m_j + n_j) mod\ n_j \\
\texttt{until}\ b_j{}^{r_j}(b_j - 1)^{n_j - r_j} \geq c_j
\end{array}
$$

Fig. 3.12. Calculation of base for multi-component equality encoded bitmap indexes for given m_j and c_j

The average number of bitmap vectors which have to be read for processing a range query [Chan and Ioannidis, 1998] is:

$$
B_{equal} = \sum_{j=1}^{d} \sum_{i=1}^{n_j} E_{r_j,i}, \text{ where}
$$

$$
E_{r_j,i} = \begin{cases} \frac{1}{b_{ji}} \left(\left\lfloor \frac{b_{ji}}{2} \right\rfloor^2 + (b_{ji} - 1) \left(\left\lceil \frac{b_{ji}}{2} \right\rceil - \frac{b_{ji}}{2} \right) \right) & : \quad b_{ji} > 2 \\ 1 & : \quad \text{otherwise} \end{cases}
$$

(3.9)

3.6.3 Range-Based Encoding

As we argued before, standard bitmap indexes do not efficiently process range queries. This section describes an approach that supports range queries more time efficient than the previous described techniques. There are different definitions of range-based encoding [Chan and Ioannidis, 1998], [Wu and Buchmann, 1998]. In this thesis we use the definition by Chan and Ioannidis.

The main idea is to set the bit of the kth bitmap vector to 1 if the value is smaller or equal the kth value. More formally, the range encoded bitmap index is calculated from the equality encoded indexes by:

$$
\overline{B}^i = \begin{cases} \overline{B}^{i-1} \vee B^i & : \quad i \geq 1 \\ B^i & : \quad i = 0 \end{cases}
$$

(3.10)

where $\overline{B}$ indicates the use of the range encoded bitmap index.

In this approach range queries of arbitrary size are processed by just reading two bitmap vectors. Figure 3.13 shows an example of a range-based index structure for the same values as in Figure 3.10. The range query $2 \leq a_1 \leq 7$ from the previous example is processed by evaluating the term:

$$
RQ([2,7]) \approx \underbrace{\overline{B}^2}_{2 \leq a_1} \wedge \underbrace{\neg \overline{B}^8}_{a_1 \leq 7}
$$

(3.11)

Since bitmap vector $\overline{B}^{11}$ equals 1 for all tuples, this vector is not stored. The space (in bitmap vectors) for range-based encoding is:

$\pi_{a_1}(R)$	$\overline{B}^{10}$	$\overline{B}^9$	$\overline{B}^8$	$\overline{B}^7$	$\overline{B}^6$	$\overline{B}^5$	$\overline{B}^4$	$\overline{B}^3$	$\overline{B}^2$	$\overline{B}^1$	$\overline{B}^0$
5	1	1	1	1	1	1	0	0	0	0	0
3	1	1	1	1	1	1	1	1	0	0	0
0	1	1	1	1	1	1	1	1	1	1	1
3	1	1	1	1	1	1	1	1	0	0	0
11	0	0	0	0	0	0	0	0	0	0	0
$\vdots$	$\vdots$	$\vdots$	$\vdots$	$\vdots$	$\vdots$	$\vdots$	$\vdots$	$\vdots$	$\vdots$	$\vdots$	$\vdots$

Fig. 3.13. Single component range-based encoded index

$$Space = \sum_{j=1}^{d}(c_j - 1) \tag{3.12}$$

The average number of bitmap vectors that are read for a range query of arbitrary size is:

$$Time = 2\sum_{j=1}^{d} \frac{b_j - 1}{b_j} \tag{3.13}$$

3.6.4 Multi-component Range-Based Encoding

The two techniques described in the Section 3.6.2 and Section 3.6.3 improve standard bitmap indexes. The multi-component bitmap index reduces the problem of low space efficiency of standard bitmap indexes for attributes with large domains. The range encoded bitmap index supports range queries more efficiently. We combine both techniques. The new structure is called a multi-component range-based encoded bitmap index. Figure 3.14 shows an example. For processing the query $2 \le a_1 \le 7$ the term

$$RQ([2,7]) \approx \underbrace{(\neg\overline{B}_1^1 \vee (\neg\overline{B}_0^2 \wedge \overline{B}_1^0))}_{2\le a_1} \wedge \underbrace{(\neg\overline{B}_1^1)}_{a_1\le 7} \tag{3.14}$$

$\pi_{a_1}(R)$	$\overline{B}_1^1$	$\overline{B}_1^0$	$\overline{B}_0^2$	$\overline{B}_0^1$	$\overline{B}_0^0$
5	1	0	1	1	0
3	1	1	0	0	0
0	1	1	1	1	1
3	1	1	0	0	0
11	0	0	0	0	0
$\vdots$	$\vdots$	$\vdots$	$\vdots$	$\vdots$	

Fig. 3.14. multi-component-<4,3> range encoded index

$$
\begin{array}{l}
n_j = 0 \\
\texttt{repeat} \\
\qquad n_j = n_j + 1 \\
\qquad b_j = \lfloor m_j/n_j \rfloor + 1 \\
\qquad r_j = (m_j + n_j) mod \ n_j \\
\texttt{until} \ (b_j + 1)^{r_j} b_j{}^{n_j - r_j} \geq c_j
\end{array}
$$

Fig. 3.15. Calculation of base for multi-component range encoded bitmap indexes for given m_j and c_j

Figure 3.15 shows the algorithm for calculation of the base of the range encoded bitmap index. This algorithm is executed for each j, $j \in \{1, \cdots, d\}$. The result defines the base in each dimension as:

$$
< \underbrace{b_j, \cdots, b_j}_{n_j - r_j}, \underbrace{b_j + 1, \cdots, b_j + 1}_{r_j} > \tag{3.15}
$$

The space (in bitmap vectors) allocated by this structure is:

$$
Space = \sum_{j=1}^{d} m_j = \sum_{j=1}^{d} \sum_{i=1}^{r_j} (b_{ji} - 1) = \sum_{j=1}^{d} ((n_j - r_j)b_j + r_j(b_j + 1)) \tag{3.16}
$$

With the given bases for the multi-component equality encoded bitmap indexes it is possible to estimate the time needed to process queries by the structure. The number of bitmaps that have to be scanned for a specific configuration according to [Chan and Ioannidis, 1998] is:

$$
B_{range} = \sum_{j=1}^{d} 2 \left(\frac{(n_j - r_j)(b_j - 1)}{b_j} + \frac{r_j b_j}{b_j + 1} \right) \tag{3.17}
$$

3.6.5 Other Compression Techniques / Combination of Bitmaps and Trees

In cases where the attribute cardinality is high many bits in the bitmap vector representation are 0. There are other than previous described techniques to compress a large number of zeros. Let us assume the space needed for storing one *tid* is 4 Bytes respectively 32 Bits. If less than $\frac{1}{32}$ of all values are 0 it is more space efficient to store a list of Tuple IDentifiers instead of a complete bitmap vector [O'Neil and Quass, 1997]. To organize the bitmap vectors and/or the tid-lists, a B-tree is used on top of the bitmap vectors/tid-lists. This technique can adapt to the actual data. If there are only a few different values, there are a few bitmap vectors. If the number of different values increases, the bitmap vectors are more sparse. Once less than a certain fraction (*e. g.* $\frac{1}{32}$) of all values are 1 it might be worth to change the index structure to a *tid*-list. However, the transformation from the *tid*-list to a bitmap representation implies some additional computation overhead.

3.7 Arrays

Arrays are efficient storage structures for dense multidimensional data. Each cell of the array holds one cell of the multidimensional data space. If the array is stored on secondary memory extensions and reorganizations of the arrays are expensive operations. Extendible arrays overcome this problem [Rotem and Zhao, 1996]. Complete reorganizations of the arrays are avoided and new data is appended to the old data. Small structures, that can be held in main memory, allow searching and retrieving of elements in the extended structure.

The mapping of array cells to blocks on secondary memory is called tiling. This tiling influences the performance of arrays stored on disks [Marques et al., 1998]. Partial sums are stored in arrays to support the calculation of range queries on aggregated data [Ho et al., 1997]. In general, arrays are used only for small databases (up to 50 GB). The approach of storing data in multidimensional structures is called *M*ultidimensional *OLAP* or MOLAP.

3.8 Summary

Data warehouses systems store large sets of data for the purpose of interactive decision support. Special techniques are applied to support fast access to the data. Due to the fact that the data cannot be completely stored on main memory, but on the secondary memory, the memory hierarchy and the mechanics of the disks influence the performance of such systems. Multidimensional index structures are developed to access the data efficiently. In detail, we presented multidimensional structures like the *R*-tree *family* and bitmap indexing techniques. For bitmap indexing techniques we presented formulars for occupied space and query processing time.

4 Mixed Integer Problems for Finding Optimal Tree-Based Index Structures

The best way to escape from a problem is to solve it.   Alan Saporta

This chapter describes an approach for finding optimal index structures by mapping the problem into a *M*ixed *I*nteger *P*roblem (MIP) and then solving the MIP using standard algorithms.

4.1 Introduction

If all data is known a priori, an approach for constructing a good in-dex structure is to create bottom-up structures from the leaves to the root [Finkel and Bentley, 1974]. Other examples for structures using this technique are the STR-tree [Leutenegger et al., 1997], packed-R-tree [Roussopoulos and Leifker, 1985] and the Hilbert R-tree [Kamel and Faloutsos, 1994]. Section 3.5.7 discusses these techniques. These approaches apply heuristics to cluster the multidimensional points according to some rule. These techniques use only the relations between single points (local optimization) and they do not reach generally a global optimum. An idea to find a global optimum with high probability is using simulated anneal-ing [Pagel, 1995].

In contrast to heuristic approaches, this chapter describes an approach that guarantees finding an optimal index structure.

4.2 Optimization Problem Parameters

The problem of finding a good clustering of points into clusters (rectangles) is mapped to a MIP and then processed with a MIP-solver. Every tuple is a point in a d-dimensional data space and every leaf node is mapped to a rectangle. Therefore, the terms tuple and points respectively leaf nodes and rectangles have similar meanings and are used interchangeable. If a tuple belongs to a certain node/cluster, its point is in the rectangle of the leaf node it belongs to. Since overlaps between rectangles are allowed, a point lying in a rectangle does not necessarily imply that its tuple must belong to the node of that rectangle. We define now all parameters needed for our approach.

M. Juergens: Index Structures for Data Warehouses, LNCS 1859, pp. 35-41, 2002.
© Springer-Verlag Berlin Heidelberg 2002

- Dimensionality of data d. Examples presented in this chapter assume the dimensionality $d = 2$. In general we assume $d \in \mathbb{N}$.
- Set P of d-dimensional points, which are to be clustered. $P = \{(p_{11}, \cdots , p_{1d}), \cdots , (p_{t1}, \cdots , p_{td})\}$.
- The cardinality of P is represented by t, ($|P| = t$). In the examples small sets with 4, 8, 12, and 16 points are used. We define $T = \{1, \cdots , t\}$.
- The number of leaf nodes or clusters is denoted by n. The number n is given as an input parameter. The set P of t tuples has to be clustered into n nodes. In the example $n \in \{1, 2, 3, 4\}$, We define $N = \{1, \cdots , n\}$.
- B_{leaf} is the maximal number of tuples per leaf node. This is the capacity of a leaf node. (In the example: $B_{leaf} = 5$).
- b_{leaf} is the minimum number of points per leaf node. (In the example: $b_{leaf} = 2$, minimum usage of nodes 40%).

The values of B_{leaf} and b_{leaf} are constraint. There cannot be more tuples than the capacity of all leaf pages and there must be enough tuples to fill the leaf pages with at least b_{leaf} tuples ($b_{leaf} * n \leq t \leq B_{leaf} * n$).

4.3 Mapping into a Mixed Integer Problem

The task is to cluster t tuples into n leaf nodes. Each leaf node contains between b_{leaf} and B_{leaf} tuples. The affiliation of a tuple to a leaf node is modeled by binary variables x_{ij}. Variable x_{ij} is set to 1 if and only if tuple j belongs to leaf node i. If tuple j does not belong to leaf node i x_{ij} is set to 0. Leaf nodes are represented by the minimum bounding boxes (rectangles) of all points belonging to the cluster. l_{ik} is the lower limit of the bounding box of cluster i in dimension k, and u_{ik} is the upper border of the bounding box of cluster i in dimension k. Figure 4.1 shows an example. Based on the above parameters we define a corresponding MIP for the leaf node level. In order to extend the model to other levels of the tree, all equations have to be applied to all other levels, too. Due to its similarity of the other relations, we do not present this here.

Objective: Minimize the sum of *margins* of all clusters:

$$\min \sum_{i \in N} \sum_{k \in \{1, \cdots , d\}} (u_{ik} - l_{ik}) \tag{4.1}$$

We mention that all u_{ik}, l_{ik}, and x_{ij} are variables of the MIP, but only the u_{ik} and l_{ik} occur in the objective function. With *margin* we denote half of the perimeter. The minimization of the sum of margins of all clusters is chosen as the objective function because this yields rather quadratic rectangles. Other objectives like *minimize overlaps of all clusters* or *minimize the area of all clusters* do not generate quadratic rectangles and have the additional

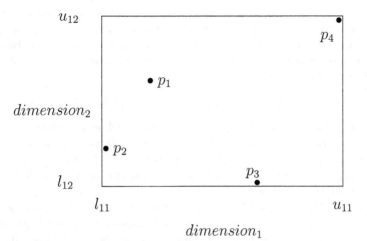

Fig. 4.1. Upper and lower bounds for MIP

drawback that they cannot be expressed as linear functions. The complexity of MIPS with non linear objectives is higher than the complexity of MIPS with linear objectives.

To guarantee that the calculated solution satisfies all necessary conditions of a tree-based index structure, the following constraints have to hold:

Constraints:
Each point p_j belongs to exactly one cluster:

$$\sum_{i \in N} x_{ij} = 1 \quad \forall j \in T \tag{4.2}$$

The number of tuples per leaf node is limited by the maximum fanout. Each cluster stores at most B_{leaf} points:

$$\sum_{j \in T} x_{ij} \leq B_{leaf} \quad \forall i \in N \tag{4.3}$$

Each cluster contains at least b_{leaf} points:

$$\sum_{j \in T} x_{ij} \geq b_{leaf} \quad \forall i \in N \tag{4.4}$$

All tuples of a leaf node are inside the bounding box of the leaf node. We check the upper limits:

$$x_{ij} p_{jk} \leq u_{ik} \quad \forall k \in \{1, \cdots, d\} \ \forall j \in T \ \forall i \in N \tag{4.5}$$

If $x_{ij} = 1$, the point j belongs to cluster i and the coordinates of point j are lower or equal the upper bounds of cluster i. If $x_{ij} = 0$, point j does not belong to cluster i and nothing is checked. In this case the left hand side equals 0 and the constraints are true for all reasonable p_{jk} and l_{ik}. We check the lower limits:

$$(1 - x_{ij})H_k + p_{jk} \geq l_{ik} \quad \forall k \in \{1, \cdots, d\} \; \forall j \in T \; \forall i \in N \qquad (4.6)$$

where $H_k \geq \max_{j \in T} p_{jk}$. If $x_{ij} = 1$, the point j belongs to cluster i and the coordinates are checked. Then $(1 - x_{ij})$ becomes 0 and the above equation remains to $p_{ij} \geq l_{ik}$. If point j does not belong to cluster i, x_{ij} is set to 0 and a "large" constant value is added to the left side of the equation and the equation is true for all p_{jk} and l_{jk}.

The fact that the lower bounds are always less than or equal to the upper bounds can be followed from Equation 4.4, Equation 4.5 and Equation 4.6. The next four equations define the domain of the used variables. All x_{ij} are binary variables:

$$x_{ij} \in \{0, 1\} \quad \forall j \in T \; \forall i \in N \qquad (4.7)$$

All p_{jk} are not negative reals:

$$p_{ij} \in \mathbb{R}_0^+ \quad \forall k \in \{1, \cdots, d\} \; \forall j \in T \qquad (4.8)$$

All l_{jk} are not negative reals:

$$l_{ij} \in \mathbb{R}_0^+ \quad \forall k \in \{1, \cdots, d\} \; \forall j \in N \qquad (4.9)$$

All u_{jk} are not negative reals:

$$u_{ij} \in \mathbb{R}_0^+ \quad \forall k \in \{1, \cdots, d\} \; \forall j \in N \qquad (4.10)$$

Equation 4.2 through Equation 4.10 define the constraints and the variables of a MIP. A solution defined by the these equations guarantees to be a valid solution. If, in addition to the constraints, the objective function defined in Equation 4.1 is minimized, an optimal solution is found.

4.4 Problem Complexity

The number of variables and constraints depends on the number of tuples t, the number of leaf nodes n, and the number of dimensions d. The time complexity of a MIP depends mostly on the number of integer variables that are defined in the MIP. This MIP contains only the binary variables x_{ij}. There are $t * n$ binary variables x_{ij}. Scientific standard algorithms solve MIPs with a branch and bound algorithm where one more integer variable increases the height of the branch and bound tree by one. Therefore, the time complexity is $O(2^{tn})$. This exponential growth implies that the algorithm cannot be used for real sized problems but only for small examples.

4.5 Model Evaluation

Although the time complexity is high, evaluation of the MIP is done for small data sets. We run experiments in order to check how the solutions calculated by the above described MIP differ from solutions found by heuristics. We apply the MIP and the R^*-tree for different numbers of tuples and clusters. We use the R^*-tree as a reference structure throughout this thesis. New techniques applied in this thesis are tested against the widely used R^*-tree.

Table 4.1. Calculated margins of R^*-tree and MIP for different configurations, R^*-tree on Sun Sparc 10 and MIP solver cplex 3.0 on Sun Sparc 4

Cluster	Points	fanout		Margin		CPU-time [sec]	
n	t	B_{leaf}	b_{leaf}	R^*	MIP	R^*	MIP
1	4	5	2	118	118	0.00	0.01
2	8	5	2	119	118	0.01	0.34
3	12	5	2	149	147	0.02	38.64
4	16	5	2	176	173	0.02	14127.84

Table 4.1 shows the results of experiments with four sets of points which are clustered into one to four leaf nodes. The results in column five and column six show that the clusterings found by the R^*-tree have approximately the same quality in terms of minimum margin as the MIP-clusterings. Therefore, heuristics as the R^*-tree are quite good in clustering data for small problems.

The costs for computing the MIP-clustering grow exponentially with the number of clusters and the number of points. Experiments show that this approach is not feasible for practical problems. The MIP is solved with cplex 3.0 running on a Sun Sparc Station-4. Better hardware and software could make the experiments faster, but for real problems, it is still slow. The R^*-tree implementation runs on Sun Sparc Station-10. The Sun Sparc Station-10 is about four times faster than the Sun Sparc Station-4. This constant factor in speed does not change the meaning of the results.

The clusterings of the first experiments with $n = 1$ and $t = 4$ found by the MIP and R^*-tree are the same and, therefore, are not graphically presented.

The left sides of Figure 4.2, Figure 4.3, and Figure 4.4 show the clusterings generated by the R^*-tree. The figures on the right side show the clusterings calculated by the MIP approach. The R^*-tree [Beckmann et al., 1990] is an heuristic approach which is applied to cluster points to the rectangles on the lowest level of the tree-structure. It calculates solutions that are nearly as good as the *optimal* solutions calculated by the the MIP approach.

More experiments with the optimizer MOPS [Suhl, 1998] show that the gap between the solution of the relaxed LP (linear problem without integer constraints) and the solution with the integer constraints is high. Therefore,

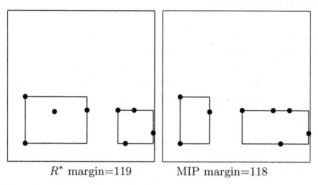

R^* margin=119   MIP margin=118

Fig. 4.2. Clustering for $t = 8$, $n = 2$

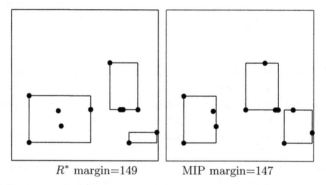

R^* margin=149   MIP margin=147

Fig. 4.3. Clustering for $t = 12$, $n = 3$

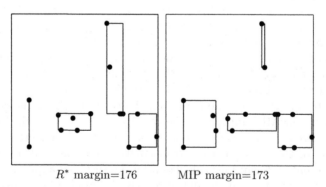

R^* margin=176   MIP margin=173

Fig. 4.4. Clustering for $t = 16$, $n = 4$

the branch and bound tree becomes large and the execution time for solving the MIP increases. More advanced techniques like column generation, could be applied to speed up moderately this technique.

4.6 Summary

This chapter investigates the creating of optimal tree-based index structures by mapping the problem of finding an optimal index structure into a MIP. The MIP is solved and the solution represents an optimal index structure according to an objective function. Experiments show that the solutions found by the MIP are only slightly better than solutions found by the heuristic R^*-tree. The time complexity of the MIP grows exponentially in the size of the input. Because of this time complexity this approach cannot be applied to real world databases. However, for small data sets this technique evaluates how closely the heuristic approaches attain its optimum. In the next chapters we will apply heuristic techniques to organize multidimensional data. Heuristic approach scale much better with the problem size than the MIP approach.

5 Aggregated Data in Tree-Based Index Structures

*I never waste memory on things that can easily be stored and retrieved from
elsewhere.*   Albert Einstein

This chapter describes an approach where aggregated data is materialized
in the inner nodes of an index structure. These data could also be calculated
from data stored in its successor nodes, but the access to aggregated data in
the inner nodes is faster than accesses to successor nodes. This concept of
aggregated data in the inner nodes is generic and is applicable to most tree-
based index structures. This chapter describes this concept of aggregated data
in the inner nodes in detail, and it shows how the algorithms are modified to
maintain and use the aggregated data. At the end of this chapter we present
results of experiments where the extended structure with aggregated data in
the inner nodes is compared with the standard structure without materialized
aggregated data.

5.1 Introduction

In this chapter we focus on range queries on aggregated data. Range queries
on aggregated data are very common in database applications such as data
warehousing. Standard index structures perform poorly for these kinds of
queries. We investigate an extension that improves the performance of index
structures for most range queries on aggregated data. The processing of point
queries will not be improved. A generic extension stores aggregated data in
the inner nodes of standard index structures and can be applied for the
majority of tree-based index structures. The main idea was presented first as
TBSAM for the case of the B-tree [Srivastava et al., 1989].

We assume that a tree-based index structure consists of two different kinds
of nodes. Leaf nodes at the bottom of the structure store the indexed attribute
values and the references to the data itself (tid-concept) [Härder and Rahm,
1999]. Non-leaf nodes (inner nodes or directory nodes) are all other nodes
including the root node. Each leaf node can hold a (not necessarily fixed)
number of leaf node entries. The directory nodes of the tree in Figure 5.1
store between two and four directory entries and the leaf nodes can store

M. Juergens: Index Structures for Data Warehouses, LNCS 1859, pp. 43-62, 2002.
© Springer-Verlag Berlin Heidelberg 2002

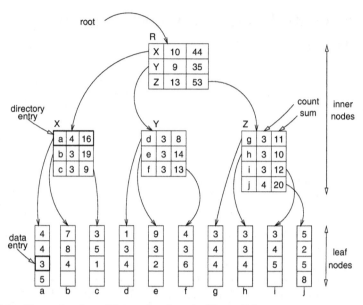

Fig. 5.1. Example of an R_a^*-tree for data in Figure 5.2

between two and four data entries. This chapter assumes that the maximum number of directory entries is fixed.

We describe how the structure is extended to speed-up the range queries on aggregated data. Only non-leaf nodes respectively inner nodes are modified but this extension does not affect entries on leaf node level. The leaf node entries keep the form $(region, ptr)$. Each non-leaf node can hold a number of directory entries. As described in Chapter 3 in standard index structures without aggregated data, the inner nodes store entries of the form $(region, ptr)$, where ptr stands for pointer and stores the link to the successor node of this entry. The variable $region$ denotes the geometric region that covers all regions of the successor node of ptr. In structures like the R-tree [Guttman, 1984] the regions are d-dimensional hyper-rectangles.

With the extension examined here, entries of the inner nodes of the tree also store aggregated data. Each directory entry is extended from a form $(region, ptr)$ to an entry of the form $(region, agg, ptr)$, where agg refers to the aggregated data. In this thesis the additional storage of the aggregated data will be called the *extension* of the index structure. For the one-dimensional case this idea is presented as TBSAM. An extension of the B-tree is described where aggregated data is stored in the inner nodes to support fast access for statistics like median or other ranking functions. For the multidimensional case this idea was presented in [Ho et al., 1997]. For multidimensional data, only the computation of a certain class of aggregate functions can be supported as we will see later.

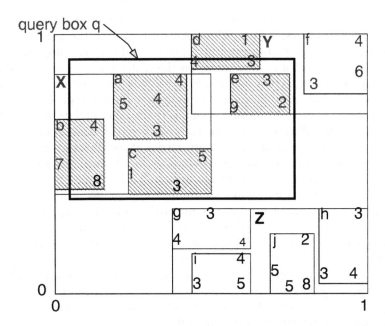

Fig. 5.2. Example data for a tree without using of aggregated data and query box q

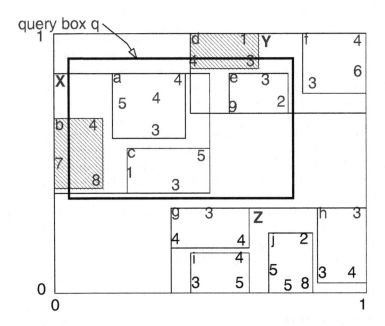

Fig. 5.3. Example data for tree using of aggregated data and query box q

We present an example to show how these extensions support range queries on aggregates. Figure 5.1 displays a tree with the aggregates sum and count attached to the directory entries. Nodes a to j are leaf nodes. Nodes X, Y, and Z are inner nodes on the first level. The root node R is on the second inner level of the tree. Figure 5.2 displays the two-dimensional data stored in this tree. Each digit represents one data item. If a directory entry refers to a *leaf* node, count contains the number of data entries of the referred *leaf*. If a directory entry points to a directory node d, count stores the sum of count values of all directory entries of the directory node d.

To see the benefits of this approach we consider range queries on aggregated data. The result of these queries are not specific tuples, but aggregated data over a set of tuples. Assume we compute the number of items contained in the query box q in Figure 5.2. The rectangles of the five hatched nodes a, b, c, d, and e intersect the query box and are accessed assuming that the data is indexed by a structure like the R^*-tree. The number of intersecting rectangles will be expressed by $Inter(q) = 5$. Rectangles a, c, and e are completely contained inside the query box. The number of these completely contained nodes will be abbreviated as $Contain(q) = 3$. The extended index structure can use the aggregated data of its inner nodes that is stored in X for leaf a and c, and in Y for node e. Only the leaf nodes b and d have to be accessed (Figure 5.3). These are the rectangles that intersect the border of the query box. The number of these rectangles is expressed by:

$$Border(q) = Inter(q) - Contain(q) = 5 - 3 = 2. \qquad (5.1)$$

We assume that each access to a leaf node corresponds to one random access to secondary memory. Therefore, only 2 accesses instead of 5 accesses are necessary in this example and 60 % of disk accesses is saved.

If necessary, the aggregate average is computed from sum and count in this example. One could try to pre-compute and store as much data as possible in the inner nodes. Adding on more aggregated data to each directory entry increases the size of each directory entry s_{dir}. The bigger the directory entries become, the fewer entries fit onto one block. This results in a smaller fanout of the directory pages. The reduced fanout may increase the height of the trees and may reduce its efficiency and this effect is discussed later in this chapter.

Figure 5.3 shows an example when aggregated data in the inner nodes yield significant performance improvements and how it affects the index structure. The remaining part of this chapter investigates under which conditions this extension of the index structure can be applied and how it influences the index structures behavior (*e. g.* operations and space). There are four aspects that must be considered when applying the extension to an index structure.

The access methods. Which access methods are *fit for aggregation*? The extension of aggregated data in the inner nodes cannot be applied for all access methods.

The aggregation functions. Values of what kind of aggregation functions should be materialized in the inner nodes of the index structure? What kind of functions are supported to compute aggregates from stored data? Not every aggregation function that can be used to pre-compute data for storage in summary tables can be applied for use to materialize data in the inner nodes of an index structure.

The operations. How must the operations performed on the index structure be changed? Insert, update, and delete operations maintain not only the data in the leaf nodes but also the aggregated data in the inner nodes. Therefore, these operations have to be modified and there is additional overhead. The range query algorithm is also changed to take advantage of aggregated data.

Additional space. How much additional space is needed to store materialized aggregated data? The benefit of having aggregated data in the inner nodes when performing queries needs additional space for redundant data.

5.2 "Fit for Aggregation" Access Method

In the next definition, the requirements are stated which must be fulfilled by a tree-based index structure so that the extension of aggregated data in the inner nodes can be applied.

Definition 5.2.1. *We call an index structure* fit for aggregation *if it fulfills the following four criteria:*

1. *The index structure consists of the two different kinds of nodes: leaf nodes and non-leaf nodes.*
2a. *Each leaf node contains data entries $data_{entry} = (region, ptr)$.*
2b. *Each non-leaf node p contains directory entries $dir_{entry} = (region, ptr)$. Each region covers at least the union of all regions of the entries ptr points to. For each entry $(region, ptr)$ the following relation must be true*

$$region \supseteq \bigcup_{dir_{entry} \in ptr} (dir_{entry}.region)$$

3. *Each node, except for the root node, has exactly one predecessor.*

By *region* there can be any sub-region of the d-dimensional data space defined. A point can also be modeled as a rectangle with zero area. It is worth mentioning that overlaps between regions of different nodes of the same level are allowed. Furthermore, no fixed size of data entries or fixed block size is assumed here to apply the extension, nor the structure need not to be balanced. However, most tree structures used in DBMSs are balanced structures. It is obvious that for access paths like hashing or bitmaps, this extension cannot be applied. The extension works in the following way: In each entry of a non-leaf node aggregated data is attached about the successors of this entry. The entries are extended to the form $(region, agg, ptr)$. agg is computed by applying an aggregation function f on the data stored in the successors. The extension of the structure is formally defined as follows:

Definition 5.2.2. *An index structure is an **extended index structure** if Definition 5.2.1 is satisfied and extended by:*

2c.   *Each non-leaf node p stores directory entries $dir_{entry} = (region, agg, ptr)$, where agg stores aggregated data about the successor nodes that is computed according to aggregation function f.*
   Let s be the node ptr is referring to. Then agg is computed by:

$$agg = \begin{cases} f(\{data_{entry}.attr | data_{entry} \in s\}) & : & s \text{ is a leaf node} \\ f(\{dir_{entry}.agg | dir_{entry} \in s\}) & : & s \text{ is a non-leaf node} \end{cases}$$

   The aggregation functions which are applicable to compute data for materialization in the inner nodes are discussed in the following section.

5.3 Materialization of Data

Section 5.2 examines how aggregated data is stored in the tree. This section investigates what aggregation functions are applicable to pre-compute data for materialization. In principal, any statistical operation can be used to compute new data from existing data. However, in hierarchical structures like trees, some functions are calculated by using pre-aggregated values while other functions can only calculated by accessing all raw data. Gray et al. classifies aggregate functions into the three categories: *distributive*, *algebraic*, and *holistic* [Gray et al., 1997].

Definition 5.3.1. *Let X be a multi-set and $X_{i, i \in \{1, \cdots, n\}}$ a partition of the multi-set X (e.g. $X = \biguplus_{i=1}^{n} X_i$). An aggregate function $f : X \rightarrow \mathbb{R}$ is <u>distributive</u> , if there exists a function g and such that, $f(X) = g(f(X_1), \cdots, f(X_n))$*

   Examples are `count`, `sum`, `min`, and `max`.

Definition 5.3.2. *An aggregation function is called <u>algebraic</u>, if it can be calculated with a fixed number of distributive functions.*

   Examples are `average` and `covariance`. These functions are not materialized in the inner nodes, but they can easily be computed by arithmetic operations on stored aggregated values of distributive functions, *e. g.* average=sum/count.

Definition 5.3.3. *An aggregation function is called <u>holistic</u> , if there is no constant bound on the size of the storage needed to describe a sub-aggregate.*

Examples are `mostFrequent`, `ranks`, and `median`. The last kind of functions we generally do not support in the multidimensional case.

However, in the one-dimensional case `ranks` or `median` functions are supported by extending the B-tree to TBSAM [Srivastava et al., 1989] if an order relation on the tree is given. We now provide an example to show how distributive aggregates are used to compute holistic functions if such an ordering can be assumed. Suppose that the data in Figure 5.4 is sorted according

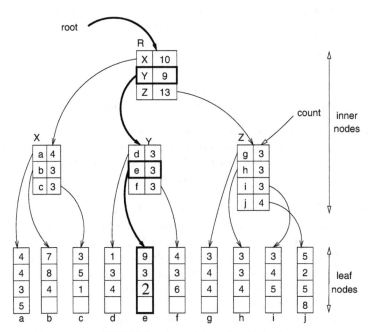

Fig. 5.4. Tree structure TBSAM and access to the 16th element

to a one-dimensional ordering and the task is to lookup the 16th element. If the count function is materialized in the inner nodes, it is possible to find the path to this element by using the count values on the upper levels. Starting from the root R, and looking at the *count* values, the 16th element has to be in the second successor Y. In node Y we have to find the path to the $16 - 10 = 6th$ element. This has to be in the second entry e of Y. In node e, it is the $6 - 3 = 3rd$ value.

Using the materialized aggregates reduces the traversal of nodes to logarithmic cost for the ranking function. Without these aggregates it would be necessary to scan the data. In the one-dimensional example the computation of a holistic function is supported by aggregated values of a distributive function.

In the remaining part of the thesis we consider multidimensional data. In the case of multidimensional data it is not possible to use aggregated data to compute holistic aggregates.

Definition 5.3.1, Definition 5.3.2, and Definition 5.3.3 classify functions into the three categories distributive functions, algebraic functions, and holistic functions. This classification is meaningful, if and only if, insert operations are considered. However, if delete and update operations are considered, the class of distributive functions must be split into two subclasses:

Definition 5.3.4. *An aggregate function* $f : X \to \mathbb{R}$ *is* _distributive additive_ *if it is distributive and there exists a function* h *such that for any* $Y \subseteq X$: $f(X \setminus Y) = h(f(X), f(Y))$.

Functions like count and sum are distributive additive.

Definition 5.3.5. *An aggregation function is called* _distributive non-additive_ *if the function is distributive but not distributive additive.*

Functions like max and min are distributive non-additive.

The distinction between distributive additive and distributive non-additive functions is important in the case of delete operations. If a tuple is removed, a distributive additive materialized aggregate can be calculated incrementally. In general, distributive non-additive aggregates have to be computed from the scratch each time a tuple is deleted or updated.

In the following approach it is assumed that only distributive (additive and non-additive) aggregates are stored in inner nodes of the index structure. Algebraic aggregates can be calculated from distributive aggregates. Holistic aggregates are not supported. In addition to the mathematical constraints of aggregation of data, the semantics of aggregation are important [Lenz and Shoshani, 1997].

We investigated what kind of functions are applicable to aggregate data for materialization. Next, we examine how the operations on an index structure have to be modified to maintain and use the materialized data.

5.4 Modified Operations

The class of tree-based index structures is viewed as an abstract data type on which operations are performed. The operations besides of search are insert, update, and delete. These algorithms are modified in order to maintain the materialized aggregates. Here we consider only distributive aggregates in the inner nodes. The query operation include point queries and range queries. Point queries will not be adapted, but range queries use the additional data to speed up the query processing time. The modification of these operations and their effect on time complexity are discussed in this section.

5.4.1 Insert Operation

For each insert operation without a split one path is traversed from the root to the leaf. During the traversal of the inner nodes the aggregated data in the nodes is updated. This works for all distributive (additive and non-additive) aggregates. The number of nodes that are touched corresponds to the height of the tree similar to a structure without aggregated data. The only difference which may yield additional overhead, is that the inner nodes may be modified. If there occurs one or more splits during the insertion phase, the aggregated data about the changed / created nodes has to be recalculated, but this does not involve additional update cost in terms of disk accesses.

5.4.2 Delete Operation

First we consider the simple case where there is a delete operation without any underflow and merging of siblings. The tree has to be traversed from the root down to the leaf node where the tuple is stored which is deleted. If additive distributive aggregates have to be updated, it can be done during the traversal from the root to the leaf node and the costs are the same as in a standard index structure. If non-additive distributive aggregates are stored, there is an additional traversal from the leaf node to the root necessary to update all inner nodes on the path. If a delete operation yields to an underflow, two siblings have to be merged and all of the aggregated data has to be updated. However, there is no additional overhead in terms of additional access to non-leaf nodes.

5.4.3 Update Operation

Update operations are exceptional in typical data warehouse applications. Therefore, we do not investigate them further. Each update can be substituted by one delete and one insert operation.

Table 5.1 summarizes the number of nodes that have to be touched for insert and delete operations when no split or merging of nodes is considered. Split and merge operations of nodes do occur only if many tuples are inserted or deleted. If a much data is changed, it is often more efficient to create a new index from scratch. For this purpose the bottom-up structures are advantageous.

5.4.4 Creating Index Structures, Bottom-Up Index Structures

As mentioned in Chapter 3, bottom-up structures like the packed R-tree [Roussopoulos and Leifker, 1985] or the STR-tree [Leutenegger et al., 1997] are well suited for *read-mostly* environments which are within the scope of this

| operation | distributive | |
	additive	non-additive
insert	h	h
delete	h	$2h$

Table 5.1. Number of nodes touched, h=height of tree

thesis. If bottom-up structures are used, the leafs of the tree are generated first, and the other levels are built from the bottom to the top. This approach is very efficient for creating a new index structure. There is no additional cost in terms of additional access to secondary memory for adding the aggregated data in the inner nodes during the creation of such a bottom-up structure.

5.4.5 Point Query Algorithm

We do not change the exact match point query algorithm by using aggregated data. Since a smaller fanout in the inner nodes of the tree might increase the height it may be necessary to traverse more nodes than in a structure without aggregated data. How the structure is affected is discussed in Section 5.6.

5.4.6 Range Query Algorithm

We modify the range query algorithm in order to use aggregated data and to speed up queries. The main idea is to avoid traversing the next level of the tree if a rectangle of a directory entry is completely contained in the query box of a range query. In this case the pre-computed materialized values stored in the directory entry are used. Based on the assumption that data entries are only points (degenerated rectangles), Figure 5.5 shows the new recursive range query algorithm. The aggregation operation is represented as f, the materialized values are stored in $dir_{entry}.agg$, and the data for materialization is stored in $data_{entry}.attr$.

The function is invoked by $calc\_agg(root, querybox)$. The function checks first if the node is a leaf node or not. In case of a leaf node for each data entry it is checked if the data entry lies in the query box. If the point lies in the query box, the value is used to calculate the aggregate. In case of a non-leaf node the function checks if the corresponding rectangle is completely contained inside the querybox q. If it is completely contained, these data can be used. Otherwise, the function calls itself recursively and proceeds to the next level of the tree.

5.5 Storage Cost

The storage of additional aggregates in the index entries reduces the fanout of the non-leaf nodes. This implies that the height of the tree may increase

```
function calc_agg(page p, region q)
initialize result;
if p is leaf node
    for all data_entry ∈ p
        if data_entry ⊆ q
            result := f(result, data_entry.attr);
else
    for all dir_entry ∈ p
        if dir_entry ⊆ query
            result := f(result, dir_entry.agg);
        else
            if (dir_entry ∩ query) ≠ ∅
                result := f(result, calc_agg(dir_entry.ptr, q));
            endif
        endif
endif
return result;
```

Fig. 5.5. Algorithm calc_aggregate for recursive range query processing

and more inner nodes are needed to hold all necessary entries. The effect of the reduced fanout on extra space for inner nodes is shown in Theorem 5.5.1. Here we assume that the fanout of the directory entries is fixed:

Theorem 5.5.1. *Let U be a tree-based index structure with n leaf nodes, u the fanout of the inner nodes, and n_u the total number of nodes. Without loss of generality we assume $n \geq u$. Let V be a second tree with n leaf nodes, reduced fanout $v > 1$ with $v < u$, and n_v the total number of leaf nodes. Let $f(u, v) = \frac{n_v}{n_u}$ be the factor the number of nodes increases when switching from structure U to structure V. This factor has an upper bound $K = \frac{1}{\left(1 - \frac{1}{v}\right)\left(1 + \frac{1}{u}\right)}$.*

Proof:
We assume having a tree-based index structure with n leaf nodes and a fanout of u. Then the total number of nodes (leaf nodes + directory nodes) is calculated by:

$$n_u \approx n + \sum_{i=1}^{\lceil \log_u n \rceil} \frac{n}{u^i} = n \sum_{i=0}^{\lceil \log_u n \rceil} \left(\frac{1}{u}\right)^i = n \frac{1 - \left(\frac{1}{u}\right)^{\lceil \log_u n \rceil + 1}}{1 - \frac{1}{u}}$$

For the tree structure with a fanout of v, the total number of nodes is:

$$n_v \approx n \frac{1 - \left(\frac{1}{v}\right)^{\lceil \log_v n \rceil + 1}}{1 - \frac{1}{v}}$$

If we switch from a tree structure with a fanout of u to a tree structure with a fanout of v, the number of nodes increases at most by factor:

$$f(u,v) = \frac{n_v}{n_u} = \frac{n\left(1 - \left(\frac{1}{v}\right)^{\lceil \log_v n \rceil + 1}\right)\left(1 - \frac{1}{u}\right)}{n\left(1 - \frac{1}{v}\right)\left(1 - \left(\frac{1}{u}\right)^{\lceil \log_u n \rceil + 1}\right)}$$

$$\leq \frac{1\left(1 - \frac{1}{u}\right)}{\left(1 - \frac{1}{v}\right)\left(1 - \left(\frac{1}{u}\right)^{(1+1)}\right)}$$

$$= \frac{1 - \frac{1}{u}}{\left(1 - \frac{1}{v}\right)\left(1 - \left(\frac{1}{u}\right)^2\right)}$$

$$= \frac{1}{\left(1 - \frac{1}{v}\right)\left(1 + \frac{1}{u}\right)} =: K$$

□

With Theorem 5.5.1 it is possible to give an upper bound for the additional space that is needed when the fanout of the inner nodes is decreased. Figure 5.6 illustrates this theorem and shows the maximum additional storage cost depending on the decreased fanout for a tree with $1,000,000$ leaf nodes. The fanout of the first tree structure is set $u = 102$ and the fanout of the second structure v is varied between 40 and 102. For a fanout of $v = 102$ of the second structure is the same structure as the first structure and no additional space is needed. For a reduced fanout of $v = 51$ only half of the directory entries fit on each directory page. Figure 5.6 shows that about one percent additional space is occupied. The additional space overhead is rather small in comparison with the whole space when the fanout is reduced.

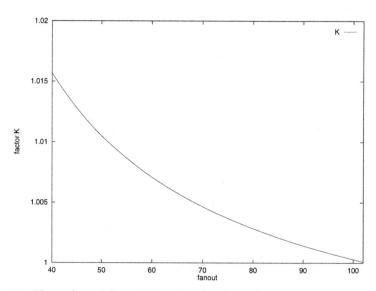

Fig. 5.6. Upper bound for additional nodes depending on reduced fanout v on x-axis ($n = 10^6$, $u = 102$)

For the above calculations it is assumed that all nodes have the same fanout. This is true for bottom-up structures, but not for index structures in general. Therefore, experimental evaluation is done with an R^*-tree. The R^*-tree with aggregated data will be denoted by R_a^*-tree [Jürgens and Lenz, 1998]. For different number of tuples an R^*-tree and an R_a^*-tree are compared and the additional storage costs is measured. In the experiments we measured on average $u = 12.8$ and $v = 9.9$ for a blocksize of $b = 512$ Bytes. We compute $K \approx 1.032$. Table 5.2 shows results from our experiments. In none of the experiments the space is increased by more than 3.05 %. These results confirm that the calculation of the upper bound K is quite close to the experimental measured value for the additional space.

Table 5.2. Factor for additional space

t	additional space $f(u, v)$
6 K	1.0296
60 K	1.0209
600 K	1.0305
1.200K	1.0273
1.800K	1.0260
6.000 K	1.0260

$(u = 12.8, v = 9.9)$

5.6 Height of Tree

Due to the decreased fanout the number of inner nodes might increase, but also the height of the tree might increase. For each processing of one level of a tree additional time is needed. Therefore, the height h of a tree is an important parameter on efficiency and is investigated. Figure 5.7 shows the height of the tree for different number of tuples t between 10^2 and 10^7 on a logarithmic scale. The fanout of the tree with aggregated data is set to $v = 51$ and the fanout of the tree without aggregation is set to $u = 102$. Figure 5.7 shows that even if the fanout of the inner nodes is cut down by half, the height of the tree is only locally increased.

5.7 Overlaps of Regions

Some multidimensional index structures (e. g. the R^*-tree) allow overlaps between different rectangles on the same level. Structures like the R^+-tree or kdb-tree avoid overlaps but no minimal fill grade can be guaranteed. To be

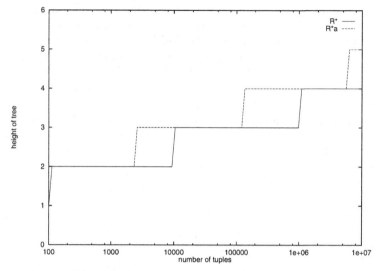

Fig. 5.7. Increased height of tree depending on the number of tuples t ($v = 51$, $u = 102$

general, the extension of aggregated data in the inner nodes is applicable to index structures that allow overlaps between rectangles of different nodes on the same level. This assumption does not restrict our approach with materialized aggregated data. A rectangle or point of a lower level can lie in more than one rectangle of an upper level. Each rectangle or point has exactly one predecessor that refers to it. In the node of this predecessor, materialized aggregated data is stored. In Figure 5.8 a small tree with two leaf nodes is shown. On the left it can be seen that point 5 lies in the rectangles of leaf nodes A and B. At the right side the tree representation shows that point 5 belongs to rectangle B. Its value is used only in the *count* and *sum* of the index entry for node B. A point might lie in two regions, but it is stored only in one leaf node. Therefore, the value of each point is used only in the computations of one aggregate on each level of the tree. The same is true for the upper levels of a tree. A region of a non leaf node can lie in more than one region of entries on higher levels of the tree, but it always belongs to exactly one node.

5.8 Experiments

In oder to check to what degree the proposed extension yields performance improvements, we perform a number of experiments. In this section we describe the experiments in detail. First we define the cost model, the physical index structures and the implementation. Then we specify the generation of

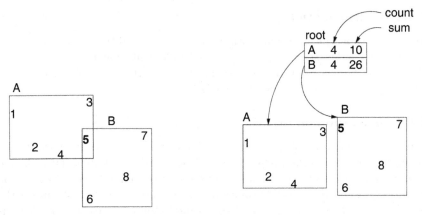

Fig. 5.8. Overlaps between region A and region B

test data and the query profile. Finally, we present the results of the experiments.

5.8.1 Cost Model

Without loss of generality we assume in this chapter that every *leaf* node is mapped to exactly one block on hard disk. If a *leaf* node is mapped to m blocks, the cost is multiplied by the constant factor m. The processing of a *leaf* node corresponds to a one-to-one access to the hard disk (or one to m). The time needed to read the block from disk and to transfer it into main memory is the critical factor. The time for traversing inner nodes and doing computations is negligible. This is due to the fact that CPUs are getting much faster and the capacity of main memories is increasing while random disk accesses remain slow.

The number of inner nodes is much smaller than the number of leaf nodes. In our experiments the number of inner nodes was usually less than 2 % of all nodes. Therefore, we assume that the inner nodes are held in main memory. In contrast is the number of leaf nodes so large that they are stored on the disk. As we mentioned in Chapter 3, disk accesses are by a factor 10^5 slower than accesses to main memory. Therefore, we consider in our cost model only the accesses to the leaf nodes.

5.8.2 Physical Index Structure

Any physical index structure structure that fulfills Definition 5.2 can be used. This chapter presents experiments where the R^*-tree is applied. The R^*-tree is very robust and a widely used reference structure to check the performance of new structures. It will be compared with the R_a^*-tree [Jürgens and Lenz, 1998].

5.8.3 Implementation

To evaluate how the extension works and how much additional space is needed for physical index structures an R^*-tree implementation based on code by Beckmann et al. is used and modified. The algorithms are coded in C and run on a SUN Ultra Sparc with 128 MB RAM.

5.8.4 Generation of Test Data

The experiments use different data sets. All data sets are two-dimensional and generated and are in the range of $[0, 1)^2$. Uniformly distributed data, skewed distributed data, and normally distributed data is used. For each distribution 10 sets of data with 1,000,000 tuples in each set are generated. We insert the ten different sets of data into ten R^*-trees and in ten R_a^*-trees. The blocksize is set to $b = 2KB$. The size of one directory entry is $s_{dir} = 20B$. Therefore, the resulting fanout of the tree without aggregated data is $u = \lfloor \frac{2048B}{20B} \rfloor = 102$. The aggregated data count and sum are materialized in the inner nodes. Therefore, the size of the directory entries increases to $s'_{dir} = 28B$. The resulting fanout for the structure with aggregated data is $v = \lfloor \frac{2048B}{28B} \rfloor = 73$.

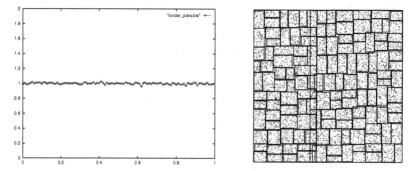

Fig. 5.9. Uniformly distributed data (left: generated density function, right: scatter diagram with rectangles of nodes of R^*-tree)

The left side of Figure 5.9 shows the empirical density function of one-dimensional uniformly distributed data generated with the C functions srand48/drand48. The right side of Figure 5.9, shows 10,000 uniformly distributed points inserted in an R^*-tree. The ten different data sets are generated with different seeds. The rectangles represent the data rectangles of the leaf nodes. The right side of Figure 5.9 shows that the rectangles have approximately the same size.

Figure 5.10 shows skewed data which is computed from uniformly distributed data by applying the function $f(x) = \sqrt{x}$, $x \in \mathbb{R}$. This holds, because $\sqrt{x}$ is the inverse function of $F(x) = \int_0^x 2y \, dy$ and $2y$ is the density function shown on the left side of Figure 5.10.

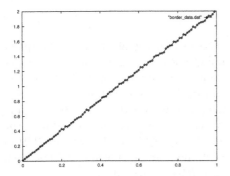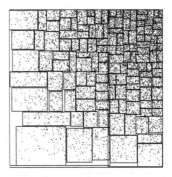

Fig. 5.10. Skewed data (left: generated density function, right: scatter diagram with rectangles of nodes of R^*-tree)

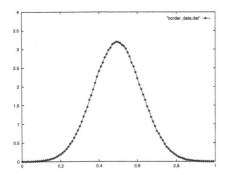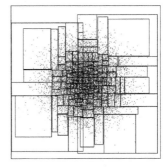

Fig. 5.11. Normally distributed data (left: generated density function, right: scatter diagram with rectangles of nodes of R^*-tree)

Figure 5.11 shows normally distributed data with $\mu = 0.5$ and $\sigma = \frac{1}{8}$. This data is generated from the uniformly distributed data by applying the Box-Muller method [Box and Muller, 1958].

5.8.5 Query Profile

For each experiment we perform a different query mix. We assume quadratic query boxes of different sizes. The area of the query boxes relative to the data space is $\{0.0005 * (2)^{\frac{i}{4}} | 0 \leq i \leq 30\}$. The distribution of the center of the query boxes is the same as the distribution of the data. *E. g.* uniformly distributed data is queried with query boxes uniformly distributed over the data space, normally distributed data is queried with query boxes normally distributed over data space. For each size of a query box and for each data set, 100 queries are processed and the average number of accesses to leaf nodes per query box is computed.

5.8.6 Results of Experiments

Figure 5.12 shows the number of disk accesses for the above described query mix for uniform distribution of data and queries. The x-axis shows the query box size in a logarithmic scale. The y-axis represents the number of disk accesses for the whole query mix. Figure 5.12 shows that for query boxes smaller than 0.001 of the data space the differences between the R^*-tree and the R_a^*-tree are rather small. For query box sizes between 0.001 and 0.01 the benefits of the R_a^*-tree are getting larger. For query boxes larger than 0.01 of the data space or more than one percent there are significant savings when using the R_a^*-tree in comparison with the R_a^*-tree, i. e. up to 85 %.

Figure 5.13 displays the number of accesses for skewed data and Figure 5.14 shows the results of the experiments with normally distributed data. These two Figures show the same trend as the data presented in Figure 5.12.

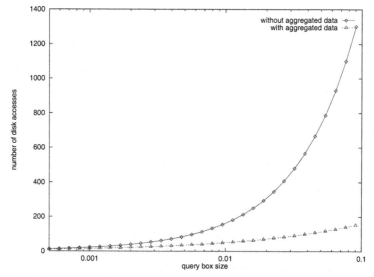

Fig. 5.12. Average number of accesses for uniformly distributed data

These experiments allow the following conclusion: The savings with the extension of the structure depend on the area of the query box. The greater the query box, the greater are the savings. The number of accesses of the tree without aggregated data is proportional to the area of the query box. The number of access of the tree without aggregated data is proportional to the perimeter of the query box. Therefore, the savings increase for larger quadratic query boxes.

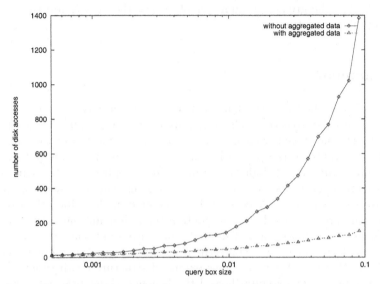

Fig. 5.13. Average number of accesses for skewed data

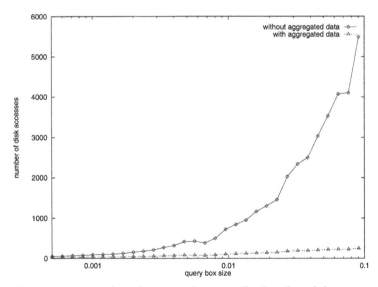

Fig. 5.14. Average number of accesses for normally distributed data

The savings also depend on the number of indexed tuples [Jürgens and Lenz, 1998]. The greater the number of tuples, the greater are the savings with the new structure.

5.9 Summary

Chapter 5 described an extension where aggregated data is stored in the inner nodes of an index structure. The aggregated data is stored in addition to the references to the successor nodes. An example shows how this extension works and how it improves the processing of range queries on aggregated data. It was defined what kind of index structures can be applied with this extension. Further investigations showed for what kind of aggregation functions can be used to pre-compute data and store it in the inner nodes. Operations on the index structure were modified to maintain the redundant data. We changed the range query algorithm and showed how much additional space-overhead is created. Experiments measured the accesses to secondary memory with a standard R^*-tree and with the new extended structure for different sizes of the query boxes. The results showed the benefits of the aggregated data in the index structures. For uniformly, skewed, and normally distributed data significant savings in disk accesses were obtained.

6 Performance Models for Tree-Based Index Structures

Make it as simple as possible, but not simpler.　　　　　Albert Einstein

In the previous chapter we showed that aggregated data in inner nodes increases the performance of tree-based index structures. Results in the previous chapter are based on experiments. We would now like to predict analytically the performance for the index structure with or without the extension. In order to design analytical models, three in literature well known performance models for index structures without aggregated data are used. We generalize the models such that they are applicable to model index structures with aggregated data [Jürgens and Lenz, 1999a].

We then introduce a fourth model that considers the distribution of data and is able to model index structures with and without aggregated data. Experiments evaluate which model is suited best for different data sets. Additionally, we apply the models to show for what kinds of data and for what kinds of queries the extension increases the performance the most.

6.1 Introduction

We take three existing models from the literature for modeling the performance of tree structures and expand these models to model index structures with aggregated data. The presented performance models work for trees, which organize the data space in multidimensional rectangles. Members of the R-tree family and many more index structures fulfill this condition. The estimated number of blocks intersecting a given query box corresponds to the number of disk accesses needed to perform the query.

6.2 Fit for Modeling

The concept of adding aggregated data to the inner nodes of an index structure specified in Definition 5.2.2 on page 48 can be applied to most tree-based index structures. In order to apply the performance models that are presented in this chapter, we refine the previous Definition 5.2.

M. Juergens: Index Structures for Data Warehouses, LNCS 1859, pp. 63-89, 2002.
© Springer-Verlag Berlin Heidelberg 2002

Definition 6.2.1. *All tree-based index structures that fulfill the* fit for aggregation *definition (Definition 5.2.2 on page 48) and that store regions as hyper-rectangles parallel to the axis are called* fit for modeling. *Each region in* (*region, agg, ptr*) *is a d-dimensional hyper-rectangle as described in Definition 3.4.2 on page 18.*

A large number of index structures fulfill this additional condition. Especially the members of the R-tree family accomplish this. Structures like the kd-tree or kdb-tree are also *fit for modeling*. Structures like the cell-tree, the SS-tree, SR-tree, or the UB-tree do not base their internal structure on rectangles but on other type of regions. Therefore, these kinds of index structures are not supported by the following performance models.

6.3 Performance Models for Access Leaf Nodes

This section presents performance models for index structures with and without aggregated data. All models consider only accesses to *leaf* nodes. The main goal of the extended structure is to minimize the number of disk accesses with minimal enlargement of the structure. Hellerstein et al. investigates the tradeoff between redundant data and access overhead in a similar context [Hellerstein et al., 1997b]. Here, we assume that all *non-leaf* nodes are stored in main memory and all *leaf* nodes are read from secondary memory. We keep the first few levels of the tree in main memory. According to Leutenegger et al. *pinning first levels in main memory gets the greatest improvements for point queries and just small improvements for range queries* [Leutenegger and Lopez, 1998]. But *pinning the upper levels of a tree in the buffer does not hurt in comparison with other buffer management policies like least recently used (LRU).* After defining these basic assumptions, we start reviewing and extending existing performance models.

The following models have some similarities. All models first estimate $Inter(q)$, the number of rectangles intersecting the query box q. In the case of an R_a^*-tree the number of completely contained rectangles is estimated by $Contain(q)$. The number of accesses of the R_a^*-tree is given with $Border(q) = Inter(q) - Contain(q)$ as shown in Equation 5.1 on page 46. In the following we assume that the data space is normalized to $S = [0, 1)^d$ where d is the number of dimensions. The size of the query box is denoted by $q = (q_1, \cdots, q_d)$. The data space in Definition 3.4.1 $O = O_1 \times \cdots \times O_d = \{0, \cdots, c_1 - 1\} \times \cdots \times \{0, \cdots, c_d - 1\}$ is transformed into $\{0, \frac{1}{c_1}, \cdots, \frac{c_1 - 1}{c_1}\} \times \cdots \times \{0, \frac{1}{c_d}, \cdots, \frac{c_d - 1}{c_d}\} = S$. Therefore, all tuples of data space O can be mapped into the data space S.

6.3.1 GRID Model

The GRID model [Theodoridis and Sellis, 1996] is the simplest of the models considered in this chapter. This model assumes that all rectangles of the leaf nodes form a regular grid. No overlaps are allowed and there is no *dead space*. That means that the whole data space is filled with hyper-rectangles. The only input parameters for the GRID model are the number d of dimensions of the data space and the number n of leaf nodes that are necessary to store all data entries. The average length of a data rectangle in the GRID model is given by:

$$\bar{r} = \frac{1}{\sqrt[d]{n}} \tag{6.1}$$

Figure 6.1 shows an example with a two-dimensional data space with $n = 64$ data rectangles (leaf nodes) and each rectangle has the length of $\bar{r} = \frac{1}{8}$ in both dimensions. We estimate the number of rectangles which intersect the query box completely by (cf. left part of Figure 6.1):

$$Inter_G(q) = \prod_{j=1}^{d} \min\left\{ \frac{q_j}{\bar{r}} + 1, \frac{1}{\bar{r}} \right\} \qquad \forall q \in 2^I \tag{6.2}$$

The number of gray shaded rectangles in the left part of Figure 6.1 corresponds to the number of blocks which are accessed when an R^*-tree is used. In this example 16 rectangles are read for a query box of size $q = (\frac{3}{8}, \frac{3}{8})$. The subscript G indicates the GRID model. The min operator in Equation 6.2 is necessary for larger query boxes. Otherwise the estimator would calculate for query boxes larger than $q = (\frac{\bar{r}-1}{\bar{r}}, \frac{\bar{r}-1}{\bar{r}})$ in at least one dimension the a wrong number of intersecting data rectangles.

Theodoridis et al. do not consider aggregated data in the inner nodes [Theodoridis and Sellis, 1996]. Therefore, we extend the GRID model. For the R_a^*-tree we estimate the number of rectangles completely contained in the query box. This is the number of white rectangles inside the gray shaded frame in the right part of Figure 6.1. Then we calculate the estimator for the number of rectangles inside the query box by:

$$Contain_G(q) = \prod_{j=1}^{d} \max\left\{ \frac{q_j}{\bar{r}} - 1, 0 \right\} \qquad \forall q \in 2^I \tag{6.3}$$

In the above example the query box contains four rectangles completely. We save this number of disk accesses when a structure like the R_a^*-tree is used in comparison with use of an R^*-tree.

The number of necessary disk accesses for an R_a^*-tree according to the GRID model is therefore the difference between the two estimators:

$$Border_G(q) = Inter_G(q) - Contain_G(q) \qquad \forall q \in 2^I \tag{6.4}$$

The GRID model has the main benefit that it is very easy and fast to compute to get a rough estimate of the needed disk accesses for data that is uniformly

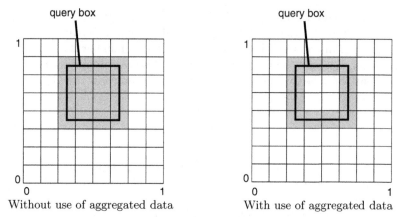

Fig. 6.1. GRID model with $d = 2$, $n = 64$, and $\bar{r} = \frac{1}{8}$

distributed over the data space. Only the number of *leaf* nodes and the size of the query box is needed. The GRID model neither considers the size of the different data rectangles nor the distribution of rectangles. The next model will overcome one of these drawbacks and use the size of the rectangles.

6.3.2 SUM Model

The SUM model is more precise than the GRID model, but it is also more complex to compute. The first part of the SUM model is developed according to two independently published approaches [Kamel and Faloutsos, 1993], [Pagel et al., 1993]. If the data space S is normalized to $[0,1)^d$ the probability for a point query to access a given rectangle equals the size of that rectangle. For example, if the size of a rectangle is 0.15 relative to the data space, the probability of a point query to access this rectangle is 15 %. According to the SUM model the probability that a rectangle intersects with the rectangle of query box q is the length of the rectangle extended in each dimension by the length of the query box in each dimension (cf. Figure 6.2). The size of the query box q and the size of rectangle i are needed for computation only. The actual positions of the query boxes and the actual positions of rectangles are not needed in these computations. Opposite to the approaches from literature where the case that the sum $q_j + r_{ij}$ can become greater than 1 is not excluded, we solve this problem by using a min-function. For each rectangle $i = 1, \cdots, n$ we calculate the probability $p_i = \prod_{j=1}^{d} \min\{q_j + r_{ij}, 1\}$, so that it intersects the query box. The sum of all these probabilities provides the exptected number of rectangles intersecting the query box q according to SUM model as:

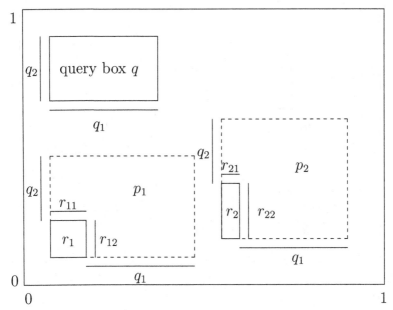

Fig. 6.2. Illustration of p_1, p_2 for SUM model

$$Inter_S^n(q) = \sum_{i=1}^{n} \underbrace{\prod_{j=1}^{d} \min\{q_j + r_{ij}, 1\}}_{p_i} \qquad \forall q \in 2^I \qquad (6.5)$$

The superscript n indicates that all n rectangles are used to calculate the expected value and the subscript S indicates that the SUM model is used.

In the second part, we extend the SUM model and consider the use of aggregated data. For a tree-based index structure with aggregated data inside the index structure we need to estimate the probability that a query box q completely contains a rectangle i (e. g. rectangles a and c in Figure 5.2 on page 45). To the best of our knowledge this measure is not presented in literature before. From Figure 6.3 one can derive $p_i' = \prod_{j=1}^{d} \max\{q_j - r_{ij}, 0\}$. To prevent $q_j - r_{ij}$ to become negative, we use the max function. The expected number of rectangles completely contained in the query box is computed by:

$$Contain_S^n(q) = \sum_{i=1}^{n} \underbrace{\prod_{j=1}^{d} \max\{q_j - r_{ij}, 0\}}_{p_i'} \qquad \forall q \in 2^I \qquad (6.6)$$

According to Equation 5.1 the expected number of blocks to be read from secondary memory is the difference between the number of nodes intersecting

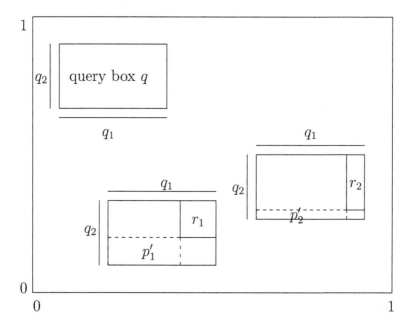

Fig. 6.3. Illustration of p'_1, p'_2

the query box and the number of nodes completely contained in the query box:

$$Border_S^n(q) = Inter_S^n(q) - Contain_S^n(q) \qquad (6.7)$$

With the given functions $Inter_S^n(q)$ and $Border_S^n(q)$ we are able to predict the number of disk accesses for a given query box for tree structures with and without materialized aggregated data in the inner nodes according to the SUM model.

6.3.3 Equivalence of GRID Model and SUM Model

The GRID model and the SUM model seem to be quite different. However, under some preconditions they area equal.

Theorem 6.3.1. *Assume that in the SUM model there are no overlaps between* leaf *nodes, the* leaf *nodes cover the whole data space (completeness), and all leaf nodes have the same size (equisize). Then it follows that* $Inter_S^n(q) = Inter_G(q)$ *and* $Border_S^n(q) = Border_G(q) \qquad \forall q \in 2^I$.

Proof:
We denote the length of a rectangle in the SUM model as r.

$$Inter_S^n(q) = \sum_{i=1}^{n} \prod_{j=1}^{d} \min\{q_j + r, 1\}$$

$$= nr^d \prod_{j=1}^{d} \min\left\{\frac{q_j}{r} + 1, \frac{1}{r}\right\}$$

$$= n \underbrace{\left(\frac{1}{\sqrt[d]{n}}\right)^d}_{=1} \prod_{j=1}^{d} \min\left\{\frac{q_j}{\bar{r}} + 1, \frac{1}{\bar{r}}\right\}$$

$$= \prod_{j=1}^{d} \min\left\{\frac{q_j}{\bar{r}} + 1, \frac{1}{\bar{r}}\right\}$$

$$= Inter_G(q)$$

Similar transformations prove $Contain_S^n(q) = Contain_G(q)$. Therefore, $Border_S^n(q) = Border_G(q)$ and the models are equivalent under the above mentioned assumptions. □

From Theorem 6.3.1 it follows that the SUM model is accurate, if the rectangles of the leaf nodes form a grid.

6.3.4 FRACTAL Model

The FRACTAL model is based on the concept of fractal dimensions [Faloutsos and Kamel, 1994]. Here, we concentrate on the number of fractal dimensions d_f of real data sets and use this concept to quantify the deviation from the uniform distribution of data.

We describe the main idea for the calculation of d_f: A grid with M squares is laid over the real dataset and for each cell of the grid it is tested, if at least one point of the real data set is contained in this cell. The number of cells that are filled with at least one point is called box count M_f. The ratio of the number of cells of the grid and the box count gives a parameter for the deviation from the uniform distribution of data.

Figure 6.4 shows points of a real data set forming a line segment. The dimensionality of the data space is $d = 2$. We lay a grid with $M = 100$ cells over the real data set. Then we count number of grid cells that contain at least one data point as box count $M_f = 10$. The following equation calculates the fractal dimension from these values by:

$$d_f = d\frac{\log(M_f)}{\log(M)} \tag{6.8}$$

In the example in Figure 6.4 the fractal dimension is $d_f = 1$. We detected a one-dimensional real data set (the line segment) in the two-dimensional data

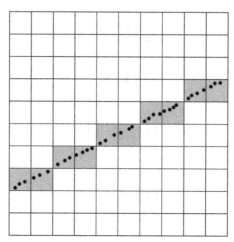

Fig. 6.4. Example of a one-dimensional figure in a two-dimensional data space, $M = 100$, $M_f = 10$, $d_f = 1$

space. The FRACTAL model applies the fractal dimension d_f to calculate the average length of data rectangles. This length is computed by:

$$r' = \frac{1}{\sqrt[d]{n}}, \tag{6.9}$$

We give an example on how d_f is used. We assume an index structure occupies $n = 9$ leaf nodes. The left part of Figure 6.5 shows the rectangles of a GRID model which assumes that the rectangles form a regular grid. The GRID model computes a value of $\bar{r} = \frac{1}{3}$ as the average length of rectangles. The FRACTAL model takes the fractal dimension d_f into account and estimates from this d_f the average length of the rectangles as $r' = \frac{1}{9}$. The size of the rectangles are shown on the right side of Figure 6.5. This example shows that the concept of fractal dimensions considers the part of the data space which the real data sets occupies. Opposite to that the GRID model assumes that the whole data space is used. Given the size of the query box $q = (q_1, \cdots, q_d)$ and the expected size of one data rectangle r' the FRACTAL model estimates the number of rectangles intersecting the query box similar to the SUM model:

$$Inter_F(q) = \sum_{i=1}^{n} \prod_{j=1}^{d} \min\{q_i + r', 1\} \quad \forall q \in 2^I \tag{6.10}$$

Similar, we calculate the number of rectangles completely contained in the query box as:

$$Contain_F(q) = \sum_{i=1}^{n} \prod_{j=1}^{d} \max\{q_i - r', 0\} \quad \forall q \in 2^I \tag{6.11}$$

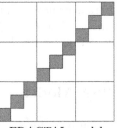

GRID model   FRACTAL model

Fig. 6.5. $d = 2$, $d_f = 1$, $n = 9$, $\Rightarrow$ GRID model: $\bar{r} = \frac{1}{3}$, FRACTAL model: $r' = \frac{1}{9}$

The number of rectangles that are accessed by an R_a^*-tree is therefore given as:

$$Border_F(q) = Inter_F(q) - Contain_F(q) \quad \forall q \in 2^I \qquad (6.12)$$

The subscript F indicates the use the FRACTAL model. Next, some equivalences between the different models are investigated.

6.3.5 Equivalence between FRACTAL Model, SUM Model, and GRID Model

We presented three different models. However, under specific conditions these models compute the same result. We formulate these equivalences in Theorem 6.3.2.

Theorem 6.3.2. *Assume that in FRACTAL model and in SUM model there are no overlaps between leaf nodes, the leaf nodes cover the whole data space (completeness), and all leaf nodes have the same size. It follows that the FRACTAL model, the SUM model, and the GRID model estimate the same values.*

Proof: If the whole data space is filled, each cell of the grid contains at least one point. Therefore, the box count $M_f = M$. From this follows $d_f = d\frac{\log(M)}{\log(M)} = d$. Therefore, $r' = \frac{1}{d_f\sqrt{n}} = \frac{1}{d\sqrt{n}} = \bar{r}$.

$$
\begin{aligned}
Inter_F(q) \quad &= \quad \sum_{i=1}^{n}\prod_{j=1}^{d}\min\{q_i + r', 1\} \\[2mm]
&\overset{r'=\bar{r}}{=} \quad \sum_{i=1}^{n}\prod_{j=1}^{d}\min\{q_i + \bar{r}, 1\} \\[2mm]
&= \quad Inter_S^n(q) \\[2mm]
&\overset{\text{Theorem 6.1}}{=} \quad Inter_G(q)
\end{aligned}
$$

Similar transformation can be done to proof $Contain_F(q) = Contain_S^n(q) = Contain_G(q)$. Therefore, $Border_F(q) = Border_S^n(q) = Border_G(q)$ and the three models are equivalent under the above defined assumptions.   □

6.4 PISA Model

This section introduces a new approach to estimate the number of disk accesses for a given range query. This model considers the actual distribution of data rectangles and the distribution of locations of query rectangles. The new model is called **Performance model for Index Structures with and without Aggregated data (PISA)** [Jürgens and Lenz, 1999a]. First we calculate the probability that two rectangles intersect with each other. Although we only present the two-dimensional case, the term rectangle refers to a multidimensional interval as noted before. We assume that the intersection probabilities in all dimensions are independent from each other. If the distributions are dependent on each other, we can still extend our model to this case. However, the model is getting more complex (cf. Section 6.8). For the case of two inde-

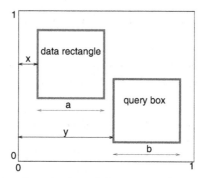

Fig. 6.6. One-dimensional projection of data rectangle and query box

pendent dimensions we consider two rectangles as shown in Figure 6.6. The two rectangles only intersect, if and only if, they intersect in each dimension. Rectangles are projected on each dimension separately. We define that the corresponding intervals A and B have length $a, b \in [0, 1)$. We consider the two intervals $A = [x, x + a)$ and $B = [y, y + b)$ where x is a realization of the random variable X distributed over $[0, 1 - a)$ and y is a realization of the random variable Y distributed over $[0, 1 - b)$, (cf. Figure 6.7). The variable x denotes the space between the leftmost point of interval A and 0. Similar the variable y denotes the space between the leftmost point of interval B and 0. We define an indicator function $f : [0, 1]^2 \rightarrow \{0, 1\}$ to decide whether two intervals A and B intersect or not:

$$f(x,y) = \begin{cases} 1 & : \quad A \text{ intersects } B \\ 0 & : \quad \text{otherwise} \end{cases} = \begin{cases} 1 & : \quad (y \geq x - b) \wedge (y \leq x + a) \\ 0 & : \quad \text{otherwise} \end{cases}$$

(6.13)

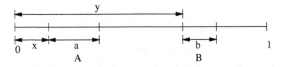

Fig. 6.7. The position of interval A of length a and interval B of length b

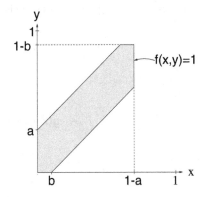

Fig. 6.8. A intersects B, $f(x,y) = 1$, in the gray shaded area

The gray shaded area in Figure 6.8 represents all possible combinations with the two intervals intersecting each other. If x and y are equal, the rectangles intersect definitely. The probability that two given rectangles intersect each other is calculated. We assume that the positions of data and query rectangles are distributed according to some parametric density function over the data space. Let d_a and d_b be the density functions of the positions of the intervals A and B. The probability that the two intervals intersect is P(A intersects B):

$$h_1(a,b) = \begin{cases} \frac{1}{(1-a)(1-b)} \int_0^{1-a} \int_0^{1-b} f(x,y)\, d_a(x)\, d_b(y)\, dy\, dx & : \quad a + b < 1 \\ 1 & : \quad \text{otherwise} \end{cases}$$

(6.14)

The PISA model uses Equation 6.14 later to adapt to different distributions. To compute the probability that a rectangle intersects the query box in multidimensional data space, h_1 is applied in all dimensions and the different probabilities are multiplied under the above assumption of dimensional independence. The total expected number of accesses is given by:

$$Inter_P^n(q) = \sum_{i=1}^{n} \prod_{j=1}^{d} h_1(q_j, r_{ij}) \quad \forall q \in 2^I \tag{6.15}$$

If aggregates in the inner nodes of the tree are available, there is no need to access *leaf* nodes whose rectangles are completely contained in the query box. We apply the same reasoning as for the derivation of $Inter_P^n(q)$. Firstly, we define an indicator function $g : [0,1]^2 \rightarrow \{0,1\}$ that decides whether one interval is completely contained in the other one:

$$g(x,y) = \begin{cases} 1 & : \quad A \text{ contains } B \\ 0 & : \quad \text{otherwise} \end{cases} = \begin{cases} 1 & : \quad (y \geq x) \wedge (y < x + a - b) \\ 0 & : \quad \text{otherwise} \end{cases} \tag{6.16}$$

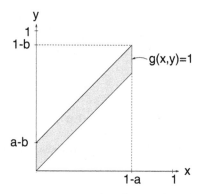

Fig. 6.9. *A contains B, $g(x,y) = 1$, in the gray shaded area*

The gray shaded area in Figure 6.9 represents the combinations of x and y values where the B is completely contained in A. If b is greater than a, it is not possible for B to be completely contained in A. The probability that two intervals intersect each other is calculated by P(A contains B):

$$h_2(a,b) = \begin{cases} \frac{1}{(1-a)(1-b)} \int_0^{1-a} \int_0^{1-b} g(x,y)\, d_a(x)\, d_b(y)\, dy\, dx & : \quad a > b \\ 0 & : \quad \text{otherwise} \end{cases} \tag{6.17}$$

The function h_2 is used to compute the expected number of rectangles that are completely contained in the query box. This formula is similar to Equation 6.15 for the case without aggregated data:

$$Contain_P^n(q) = \sum_{i=1}^n \prod_{j=1}^d h_2(q_j, r_{ij}) \quad \forall q \in 2^I \tag{6.18}$$

Equation 6.15 and Equation 6.18 consider the distribution of the rectangles and the actual distribution of the query boxes. Next, we apply the PISA model to a structure like the R_a^*-tree. We calculate the expected number of accesses as the difference of the two previously calculated functions:

$$Border_P^n(q) = Inter_P^n(q) - Contain_P^n(q) \quad \forall q \in 2^I \tag{6.19}$$

6.5 Computational Efficiency of SUM Model and PISA Model

With a large number of rectangles, the performance measures $Border(q)$ of SUM model and PISA model are expensive to compute, because we have to compute the actual size of each rectangle. One idea to speed-up computation is to assume that all rectangles are quadratic and have the same size. The average length $\tilde{r}$ of all rectangles is given by:

$$\tilde{r} = \frac{1}{n} \sum_{i=1}^n \tilde{r}_i \quad \text{with} \quad \tilde{r}_i = \sqrt[d]{\prod_{j=1}^d r_{ij}} \tag{6.20}$$

If $\tilde{r}$ is used to get *a faster to compute* expected number of inner blocks according to the SUM model, it follows:

$$Contain_S^1(q) = n \prod_{j=1}^d \max\{q_j - \tilde{r}, 0\} \quad \forall q \in 2^I \tag{6.21}$$

The superscript 1 indicates that just one rectangle (the *average* rectangle) represents all rectangles. One could argue that this simplification works only well for data where all rectangles have approximately the same size, i.e. standard deviation is neglectable.

Another way of refining the model is to classify all rectangles into k different size classes. This is done in the following way: we transform each rectangle to a square having the same area as the rectangle. The length of this square classifies the rectangle as follows:

Definition 6.5.1. *Let k be the number of different classes. The number of rectangles belonging to class l is given by:*

$$u_l = \left| \left\{ i \mid i \in \{1, \cdots, n\} \wedge \frac{l}{k} \le \tilde{r}_i < \frac{l+1}{k} \right\} \right|, \quad l \in \{0, \cdots, k-1\} \tag{6.22}$$

Figure 6.10, Figure 6.11, and Figure 6.12 show histograms for the three different data sets. The number of classes is set to $k = 100$, which is equivalent to a class width of $\frac{1}{k} = 0.01$.

The histograms show that less than the first 10 values represent the distribution of the length of the rectangles.

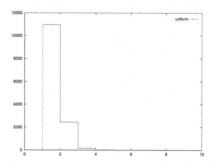

Fig. 6.10. Histogram of number of rectangles for uniformly distributed data

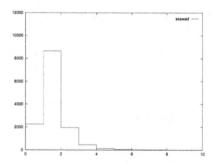

Fig. 6.11. Histogram of number of rectangles for skewed data

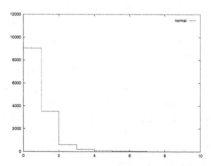

Fig. 6.12. Histogram of number of rectangles for normally distributed data

Each class l is represented by a rectangle with equal length in all dimensions. The length is the center of the interval $\left[\frac{l}{k}, \frac{l+1}{k}\right)$. Having the size of the representative rectangle and the number of rectangles of each class, the estimator for inner nodes according to SUM model is:

$$Contain_S^k(q) = \sum_{l=0}^{k-1} u_l \prod_{j=1}^{d} \max\left\{q_j - \frac{l+0.5}{k}, 0\right\} \quad \forall q \in 2^I \qquad (6.23)$$

The superscript k shows that k classes are used. In this chapter the SUM model and PISA model are used in three different *precision modes*:

- The 1-rectangle case. The *average* rectangle according to Equation 6.20 represents all rectangles (*e. g. Contain*$_S^1$ in Equation 6.21).
- The k-rectangle case. We map every rectangle into exactly one out of k classes. Each class is represented by one rectangle (*e. g. Contain*$_S^k$ in Equation 6.23).
- The n-rectangle case. Here we use the actual size of each rectangle. (*e. g. Contain*$_S^n$ in Equation 6.6).

The measures $Inter_S^1$, $Contain_S^k$, $Inter_P^1$, $Contain_P^1$, $Inter_P^k$, and $Contain_P^k$ are defined analogously.

6.6 Adapting PISA Model to Different Distributions

This section shows how PISA is adapted to different distributions. We will focus on uniform, skewed, and normal distributions to show in detail how the model is adaptable.

6.6.1 Uniformly Distributed Data

We start to show the flexibility of PISA model with uniformly distributed data. Uniformly distributed data is shown in Figure 5.9 on page 58. The density functions $d_a(x)$ and $d_b(y)$ with parameter constraints $0 \le a, b < 1$ are:

$$d_a(x) = \begin{cases} \frac{1}{1-a} & : \quad 0 \le x \le 1-a \\ 0 & : \quad \text{otherwise} \end{cases} \qquad (6.24)$$

$$d_b(y) = \begin{cases} \frac{1}{1-b} & : \quad 0 \le y \le 1-b \\ 0 & : \quad \text{otherwise} \end{cases} \qquad (6.25)$$

From Equation 6.14 we get the probability that two intervals intersect [Lenz and Jürgens, 1998]:

$$h_1(a, b) = \begin{cases} \frac{a+b-a^2-b^2-ab}{(1-a)(1-b)} & : \quad a+b < 1 \\ 1 & : \quad \text{otherwise} \end{cases} \qquad (6.26)$$

The probability that one interval completely contains the other interval is computed by combining Equation 6.17 and Equation 6.25 to:

$$h_2(a,b) = \begin{cases} \frac{a-b}{1-b} & : \quad a > b \\ 0 & : \quad \text{otherwise} \end{cases} \tag{6.27}$$

Equation 6.15 on page 74 for $Inter_P^n(q)$ and Equation 6.18 on page 75 for $Border_P^n(q)$ allow us to predict the performance of the index structures with and without aggregates in the structure for a given query box size.

6.6.2 Skewed Data

Next, we investigate how PISA can be adapted to skewed data, cf. Figure 5.10 on page 59. Its density function is given by:

$$d_a(x) = \begin{cases} \frac{2x}{1-a} & : \quad 0 \le x \le 1-a \\ 0 & : \quad \text{otherwise} \end{cases} \tag{6.28}$$

$$d_b(y) = \begin{cases} \frac{2y}{1-b} & : \quad 0 \le y \le 1-b \\ 0 & : \quad \text{otherwise} \end{cases}$$

The empirical one-dimensional density function can be seen in the left part of Figure 5.10 on page 59. The distribution of the rectangles is presented in right part of Figure 5.10. Most points are in the upper right corner of the data space.

We use Equation 6.14 and the definition of d_a and d_b in Equation 6.28 to calculate the probability that two intervals intersect each other (for $a+b < 1$):

$$\begin{aligned} h_1(a,b) = \quad & \frac{4}{(1-a)^2(b-1)^2} \left(\frac{b^2}{2} - ab^2 + \frac{3a^2b^2}{4} - b^3\frac{4ab^3}{3} \right. \\ & + \frac{7b^4}{12} + \frac{1}{3}(1-a-b)^3(a+b) - \frac{1}{3}b^3(a+b) \\ & \left. + \frac{1}{4}(1-a-b)^2(a^2-b^2) - \frac{1}{4}b^2(a^2-b^2) \right) \end{aligned} \tag{6.29}$$

Similarly we combine Equation 6.17 and the definition of d_a and d_b to derive the probability that one interval contains the other one for skewed data as (for $a > b$):

$$h_2(a,b) = \frac{\frac{4}{3}(1-a)^3(a-b) + (1-a)^2(a-b)^2}{(1-a)^2(b-1)^2} \tag{6.30}$$

Figure 6.13, Figure 6.14, and Figure 6.15 illustrates the two-dimensional case with respect to h_1. Figure 6.13 shows the two-dimensional density function $d_{a,b}(x,y) = d_a(x) * d_b(y)$. Figure 6.14 displays the indicator function

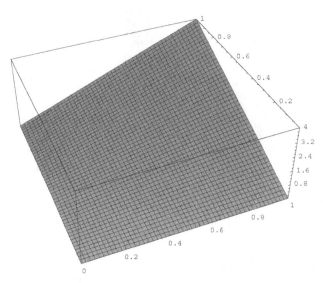

Fig. 6.13. Two-dimensional distribution $d_{a,b}(x,y) = d_a(x) * d_b(y)$ (over $[0,1]^2$ skewed data)

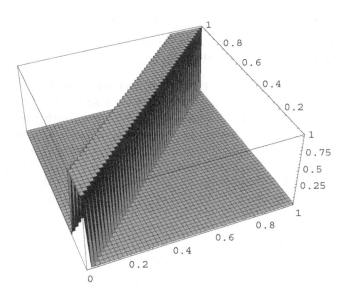

Fig. 6.14. Function $f(x,y)$

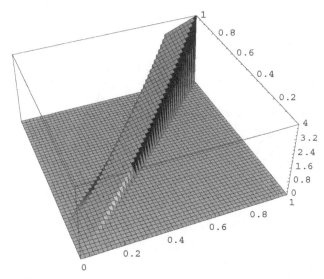

Fig. 6.15. $d_{a,b}(x, y) * f(x, y)$

$f(x, y)$. Figure 6.15 represents the integrand of Equation 6.17 as a the product of the functions $f(x, y) * d_{a,b}(x, y)$. The volume under this function is the result of the integral which is calculated as h_2.

For uniformly distributed data and for skewed data we can compute the performance measures $Border(q)$ as closed expressions.

6.6.3 Normally Distributed Data

Next, we adapt the PISA model to 'bell-shaped' normal distributed data. The normal distribution is a symmetric distribution with no closed expression for its distribution function. The test data is generated with the Box-Muller method [Box and Muller, 1958]. To standardize normal distributed random almost on $[0, 1]$ the functional parameters $\mu = \frac{1}{2}$ and $\sigma = \frac{1}{8}$ are chosen. The left side of Figure 5.11 on page 59 shows the empirical distribution of one-dimensional data. The right side of Figure 5.11 shows the distribution of the rectangles when normally distributed points are indexed by an R^*-tree. The density functions are ($\mu \in \mathbb{R}$, $\sigma \in \mathbb{R}_+$):

$$d_a(x) = \frac{1}{\sqrt{2\pi}\sigma} e^{\frac{-(x-\mu)^2}{2\sigma^2}} \qquad (6.31)$$

$$d_b(y) = \frac{1}{\sqrt{2\pi}\sigma} e^{\frac{-(y-\mu)^2}{2\sigma^2}} \qquad (6.32)$$

Equation 6.14 and Equation 6.17 cannot be solved analytically if d_a and d_b are the normal density functions. Therefore, we apply numeric approximation and approximate the distribution functions by a polynome from [Ibbetson, 1963]. Further approximations are necessary in order to compute the integrals in Equation 6.14 and Equation 6.17. Appendix B on page 123 presents these computations in detail.

$$h_2(a, b) = \frac{1}{2}(U(a, b) + L(a, b)) \tag{6.33}$$

The two functions $U_{a,b}$ and $L_{a,b}$ are shown in Equation B.1 and Equation B.4 on page 124. They are upper and lower bounds of function h_2. Therefore, h_2 is approximated by the average of both values.

6.7 Model Evaluation

This section shows the results of model evaluation using the R^*-tree and R_a^*-tree as physical data structures. The R^*-tree is chosen as a representative of multidimensional tree-based index structures. The R^*-tree is a balanced structure, well known for its robustness and ability to adapt well to different data distributions. We compare results of model evaluation and measurements. The experiments were run with uniformly, skewed, and normally distributed data. In each of the following experiments we generated ten different trees with 1,000,000 tuples in each tree. The maximum fanout is $B_{leaf} = 102$ and the minimum fanout is $b_{leaf} = 41$. The average fanout is approximately 70. We assume quadratic query boxes and the size of the query box varies between 0.05 % and 6.4 % of the data space. Larger query boxes are not of interest, because the use of an index structure is slower than a sequential scan of the whole data set if more than 7 % of all leaf nodes have to be accessed.

Figures 6.16 to 6.21 use half-logarithmic scales. The x-axis represents the size of the query box relative to the whole data space. The y-axis shows the percentage deviation:

$$Y_e = \frac{|\text{modeled values} - \text{measured values}|}{\text{measured values}} * 100 \tag{6.34}$$

A graph with stars shows the deviation of the GRID model and the a graph with diamonds represents the deviation of the FRACTAL model. The graphs of the SUM model are marked with triangles and the results of PISA model are labeled with small squares. SUM model and PISA model use three precision modes as described in Chapter 6.5.

6.7.1 Uniformly Distributed Data

Figure 6.16 presents the percentage error Y_e for the R^*-tree for uniformly distributed data. The SUM model is slightly better than the PISA model.

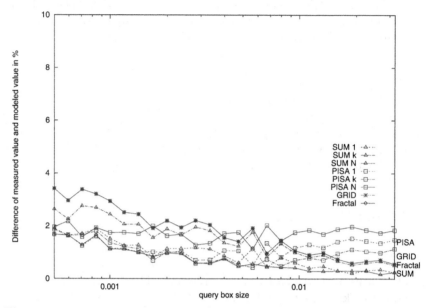

Fig. 6.16. Percentage of error Y_e of R^*-tree for uniformly distributed data

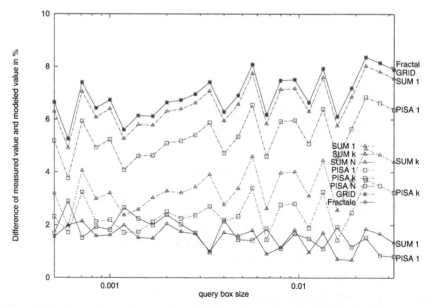

Fig. 6.17. Percentage of error Y_e of R_a^*-tree for uniformly distributed data

Figure 6.17 shows the deviations for the R_a^*-tree. The PISA model is more precise than the SUM model, but more important than the model is the precision mode that is used in the experiments. However, we think that for uniformly distributed data all models are sufficiently precise, *i. e.* the percentage error for R^*-tree is less than 4 % and the percentage error for R_a^*-tree is less than 8 %.

6.7.2 Skewed Data

For skewed data the results are shown in Figure 6.18 for the R^*-tree and in Figure 6.19 for the R_a^*-tree. The PISA model is more precise than GRID model, FRACTAL model, or SUM model. The precision mode has very little influence on the results. In Figure 6.18 the SUM model and GRID model are very close to each other and have an error rate of 35 % while the PISA model has an error of approximately 5 % for the R^*-tree. Evidently the PISA model is significantly better than the other models in case of an R_a^*-tree.

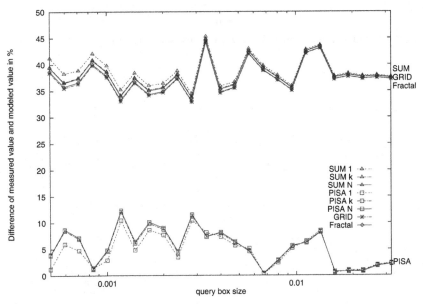

Fig. 6.18. Percentage of error Y_e of R^*-tree for skewed data

6.7.3 Normally Distributed Data

Figure 6.20 and Figure 6.21 show results for normally distributed data. The PISA model is much more precise than the other models. For the R^*-tree the

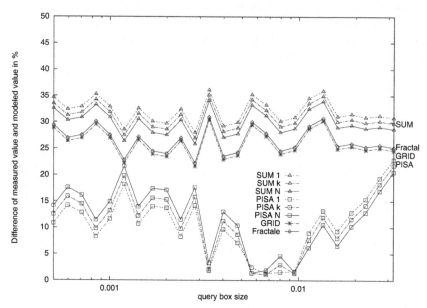

Fig. 6.19. Percentage of error Y_e of R_a^*-tree for skewed data

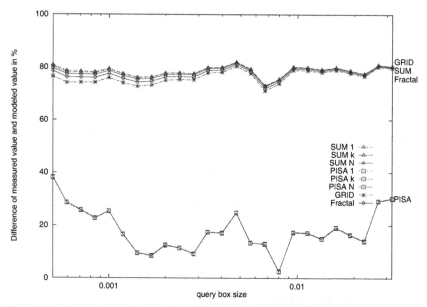

Fig. 6.20. Percentage of error Y_e of R^*-tree for normally distributed data

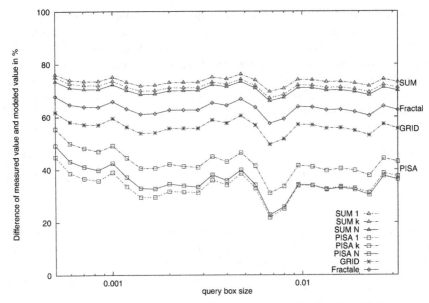

Fig. 6.21. Percentage of error Y_e of R_a^*-tree for normally distributed data

PISA model has error rates of approximately 20 % while the SUM and GRID model have error rate of 80 % (!). Notice that for this model the precision mode has nearly no influence. It is much more important to choose the right model. For the R_a^*-tree the PISA model reaches error rates of 40 %, but is clearly more precise than the GRID or SUM model.

The evaluation of the models show that PISA model dominates all the other models. This is true due to the fact that PISA model considers the actual distribution of data and queries. The SUM model and the FRACTAL model assume implicit uniformly distributed data. Usually, real world data is not uniformly distributed. Therefore, we believe that the PISA model has a great impact on performance evaluations on real world data.

6.8 PISA Model for Dependent Data

One assumption of the PISA model is that the joint distribution of the data can be modeled by marginal distribution on each dimension separately, i.e. independently. In many real applications this assumption does not hold and correlations between different dimensions in the data exist. We show how the PISA model is extended to use joint distributions. In this chapter, the two-dimensional case is considered only, but extension is straightforward and can be applied to any fixed number of dimensions.

Let $d_a(x, y)$ be the two-dimensional density function of the location of data rectangles, and let $d_b(x, y)$ be the two-dimensional density function of the location of the query boxes. Let r_1, r_2 be the length and width of the data rectangle, and let q_1, q_2 denote the length and width of the query box. The probability h_1 that rectangles intersect is computed similarly as for the one-dimensional case. If $(q_1 + r_1 \leq 1) \wedge (q_2 + r_2 \leq 1)$ and $(0 \leq r_1, r_2, q_1, q_2 < 1)$ the probability is calculated as:

$$h_1(r_1, r_2, q_1, q_2) = \qquad\qquad\qquad\qquad\qquad\qquad\qquad (6.35)$$
$$\frac{\int_0^{1-r_1} \int_0^{1-r_2} \int_0^{1-q_1} \int_0^{1-q_2} f(x_1, x_2) f(y_1, y_2) d_a(x_1, y_1) d_b(x_2, y_2) dy_2 dx_2 dy_1 dx_1}{(1 - r_1)(1 - r_2)(1 - q_1)(1 - q_2)}$$

If a structure like the R_a^*-tree is used, we need the probability h_2 that the query box contains completely a given rectangle. If $(q_1 > r_1) \wedge (q_2 > r_2)$ and $(0 \leq r_1, r_2, q_1, q_2 < 1)$, the probability is:

$$h_2(r_1, r_2, q_1, q_2) = \qquad\qquad\qquad\qquad\qquad\qquad\qquad (6.36)$$
$$\frac{\int_0^{1-r_1} \int_0^{1-r_2} \int_0^{1-q_1} \int_0^{1-q_2} g(x_1, x_2) g(y_1, y_2) d_a(x_1, y_1) d_b(x_2, y_2) dy_2 dx_2 dy_1 dx_1}{(1 - r_1)(1 - r_2)(1 - q_1)(1 - q_2)}$$

If $(q_1 \leq r_1) \vee (q_2 \leq r_2)$ the rectangle is too small to be completely contained inside the query box and we set $h_2(r_1, r_2, q_1, q_2) = 0$.

6.9 Extension of Models

The models are based on the assumption that the leaf nodes are stored on a disk system while all inner nodes are held in main memory. The access to the secondary memory is about factor 10^5 slower than accessing main memory. Therefore, the cost models for the above described models consider only the leaf node level. In some applications this assumption does not hold and we have to extend the model to other levels of the tree.

Assume the tree has a height of h and the first j levels ($j \in \{0, \cdots, h-1\}$) are stored in main memory. Then $h-j$ levels are stored on secondary memory. For this case the above described models are applied for each level. Altogether the models are applied $h - j$ times and the results of all levels are summed up to get the total estimator.

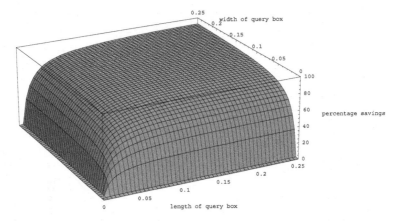

Fig. 6.22. Percentage savings of disk accesses of R_a^*-tree and R^*-tree by length and width of query box (PISA model, 40.000 leaf nodes with uniformly distributed data)

6.10 Applications of Models

In this section we investigate under which conditions (i. e. size, form, number of dimensions) the use of aggregated data yields better performance compared to neglecting aggregated data.

6.10.1 Savings of R^*_a-tree Depending on the Query Box Size and Form

Figure 6.22 shows the estimated savings in percent of the R_a^*-tree over the R^*-tree for different sizes of the query box. The x- and y-coordinates are the length and the width of the query box. The z-coordinate shows the savings in percent. The R_a^*-tree outperforms the R^*-tree for large quadratic query boxes. Points close to the x-axis or y-axis represent thin or short queries, so called 'spaghetti' queries. For this class of queries there is no or only small benefit of using the R_a^*-tree, whereas for large quadratic queries the savings are significant. Notice the scale of Figure 6.22. Only for very thin of very short query boxes are there no savings using the R_a^*-tree.

6.10.2 Savings of R^*_a-tree Depending on the Number of Dimensions

Figure 6.22 shows that savings depend on the size and form of the query box. It is evident that not only the query box sizes influences savings. The data also heavily influences the performance of the index structure.

Figure 6.23 shows the percentage of savings of the structure with and without aggregated data for different number of dimensions. It is assumed

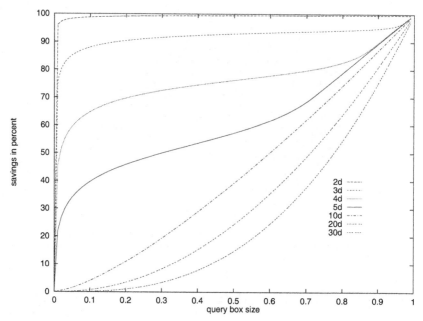

Fig. 6.23. Savings of accesses for different number of dimensions

that there is an index structure with $n = 10^6$ leaf nodes and the number of dimensions is varied. We use only quadratic query boxes and vary the size of the query box relatively to the data space. Figure 6.23 shows that the structure is efficient for few dimensions, i.e. $d \leq 5$. For the two and three-dimensional case the structure rapidly reaches savings of close to 90 %. For up to 5 dimensions there can be an significant performance improvement gained with the aggregated data. For more than ten dimensions the improvements are rather small. As is well known the R^*-tree is not very efficient for high dimensional data. Our extension to the R^*-tree with aggregated data is most efficient in cases where the R^*-tree is efficient. Consequently this extension should be applied in case of less than five dimensions and large query boxes.

6.11 Summary

This chapter discussed models for non-extended and models for extended multidimensional index structures. The key idea of the extension is to store materialized aggregates in the inner nodes of the tree structure. The use of this materialized data reduces the processing time of range queries.

To estimate the performance of multidimensional index structures various existing performance models are studied and extended. A new **P**erformance model for **I**ndex **S**tructures with and without **A**ggregated data (PISA) is presented. We show how PISA can be adapted to uniformly, skewed, and normally distributed data. The R^*-tree and R^*_a-tree is taken as reference index structures to evaluate the accuracy of the models. The evaluation of the models confirms that the PISA model is more precise than other existing models. Applications of models show for what kind of data and for what kind of queries the extension of the R^*-tree to the R^*_a-tree is relative efficient.

7 Techniques for Comparing Index Structures

It is evident from the preceeding chapters that the various index structures accelerate query processing differently. For some kinds of queries and data certain classes of index structures perform fast, while for others other classes of index structures are more efficient. Sarawagi makes qualitative propositions for a comparison of index structures [Sarawagi, 1997]. The performance of query processing depends on various parameters which influence the query execution time. We focus on a set of nine parameters. Two approaches are presented to support the decision making process which index structure should be applied. The first approach is based on classification trees. The second approach uses an aggregation method. Both approaches are applied to two classes with altogether four distinct index structures: a tree-based index structure without aggregated data, a tree-based index structure with aggregated data and two bitmap index structures. This chapter closes with results of a detailed performance study.

7.1 Introduction

Most performance investigations of index structures only consider one or two parameters at at time such as the blocksize b or the number of dimensions d. However, the performance of index structures depends on more than one or two parameters and there exist interactions between them. However, this chapter concentrates on a set of nine different parameters to compare index structures for processing range queries. The nine parameters are carefully chosen to describe data, queries, system behavior, and disk technology. We think that the nine parameters describe the experimental setup sufficiently precise. However, if more parameters should be needed, the described approaches can be extended easily to consider additional parameters.

7.2 Experimental Parameters

7.2.1 Data Specific Parameters

Data specific parameters are described below:

M. Juergens: Index Structures for Data Warehouses, LNCS 1859, pp. 91-111, 2002.
© Springer-Verlag Berlin Heidelberg 2002

Dimensionality. Dimensionality $d \in \mathbb{N}$ of the data denotes the number of attributes. For the task of indexing eight-dimensional data a different index structure may be better suited than for indexing one or two-dimensional data.

Number of stored tuples. The number $t \in \mathbb{N}$ of tuples influences the performance of different structures. The R_a^*-tree improves in comparison with the R^*-tree if the number of indexed tuples increases [Jürgens and Lenz, 1998].

Cardinality of data space. The cardinality c of the range of an attribute is the number of different values an attribute may have. Gender has three possible values (male, female, NULL). Attributes like social security number or telephone number may have millions of different values. For attributes like gender different index structures are better suited than for attributes like social security number or telephone number. We assume that the attribute space is normalized in the range $[0, 1)$ and that the attribute cardinality is the same in all dimensions. This assumption simplifies the model. It is relaxed later to make the experiments more realistic. Then the cardinality is denoted by c_j, $(j \in \{1, \cdots, d\})$.

The distribution type of data may be another parameter (*e. g.* uniform versus not uniform distribution). This Chapter does not consider this parameter. However, the described techniques can easily be extended to take other distributions into account. In this case the models for the tree structures are changed according to the PISA model (cf. Chapter 6). This chapter assumes uniformly distributed data. Note, that models for bitmaps are not affected by non-uniform distributions of data.

7.2.2 Query Specific Parameters

Query specific parameters hold information about the queries processed by the system. In our approach we concentrate on range queries. Point queries are expressed as range queries with query box size $qs = 0$. In order to have only scalar values as parameters we assume that there are only range queries which can be described with the two scalar values query box size qs and query box dimensions qd:

Query box size. The size of the query box $qs \in \mathbb{R}$ is a fraction of the data space and is denoted by $qs \in [0, 1]$. A value of $qs = 0.04$ means that the query box fills 4 percent of the data space.

Query box dimensions. The query box dimension parameter $qd \in \mathbb{N}$ denotes the number of attributes occurring in a given range query. Assume that a five-dimensional index is built ($d = 5$) but that the query is restricted to two dimensions. In this case qd is set to 2. The size of the query box in the first qd dimensions is set to $q_i = qs^{\frac{1}{qd}}$ for all $1 \leq i \leq qd$. The size of the query box in the remaining dimensions is set at $q_i = 1$

for all $qd < i \leq d$. This means there are no restrictions or predicates in the remaining dimensions. Example: Assuming that the size of the query box is $qs = 0.04$ and the query box dimensions parameter is $qd = 2$. Then the shape of the query box is calculated with the above given rule as $q = (0.2, 0.2, 1, 1, 1)$. This limits the model to certain shapes of query boxes, but it allows the model to work with scalar values as input parameters.

It is assumed that the locations of the query boxes are uniformly distributed over the data space. If this assumption does not hold the model can be adapted as presented in the PISA model in Chapter 6.

7.2.3 System Specific Parameters

System specific parameters are parameters which are chosen by the database administrator (DBA) of a system. We assume that the DBMS has its own access to the disk system and does not use the I/O functions of the operating system:

Blocksize. The blocksize $b \in \mathbb{N}$ is the number of KB that are read with one disk access. Whenever data is requested from secondary memory at least one whole block is read and is transfered. The size of this block is given by the blocksize b in KB.

Scale factor. Due to the fact that the access time, and not the available disk space, is the limiting factor, controlled redundancy of stored data is accepted in order to be more time efficient. This is especially true in the context of data warehouse systems where materialized views occupy a large portion of disk space. In general, the more data is materialized the more queries are answered without accessing base data and the faster the system responses become. Some index structures have the same property in that they can trade space and time. For example, the more space is occupied by bitmap indexes, the more time efficient structures are generated. We use bitmap indexes that are *time optimal under given space constraints* [Chan and Ioannidis, 1998]. Bitmap indexes are characterized by a scale factor $sf \in \mathbb{R}$ times the space occupied by the tree structures. *E. g.* a scale factor of $sf = 2$ means that the bitmap indexes can occupy twice the space used by trees.

7.2.4 Disk Specific Parameters

Besides inner nodes of R^*-trees index structures are usually not stored in main memory but in secondary memory. If a query is processed with an index structure, that structure (or part of it) has to be read from secondary memory and transfered into main memory. Many approaches compare index structures by only counting the number of external I/Os. Our approach does not neglect the fact that reading blocks sequentially is much faster than reading blocks randomly.

The behavior of disks is modeled by two parameters:

Bandwidth. The Bandwidth $bw \in \mathbb{R}^+$ of a disk is the speed [MB/s] with which the disk can read data and transfer it into main memory. Since data is stored more and more densely on the disks over time, this speed increases by approximately 40 % per year [Bitton and Gray, 1998], [Patterson and Keeton, 1998]).

Latency time. The second parameter is the average time t_l of positioning the read/write heads and to start reading the needed data. This time is the latency time $t_l \in \mathbb{R}$ of a disk system. On page 16 we defined latency time=SeekTime+RotationTime/2. This parameter depends mainly on the rotation speed of the disk. The rotation speed does not increase at the same rate as the bandwidth bw. It increases only by approximately 8 % per year [Bitton and Gray, 1998], [Patterson and Keeton, 1998].

The time for a random disk access t_r and the time for a sequential disk access is calculated from the above parameters as shown in Section 3.3 on page 16. The fact that the bandwidth bw increases much faster than the latency time t_l, decreases, widens the gap between a sequential and a random block access. With today's (2000) disk technology, using a reasonable large blocksize it is ten to twenty times faster to read a sequential block than a random block. In five years, this factor will probably be increased by 30 to 70. One can argue that by then index structures will only be of limited use, because sequential scans will be faster for most queries than using index structures. This is true if the amount of data is kept fixed. But the capacity of disks (and the amount of stored data) increases even faster than the bandwidth. Therefore, the time for scanning a whole disk increases, and it will still be necessary to index data. However, the index structures will have to adapt according to the changed parameters.

7.2.5 Configuration

For our experimental setups we group the above defined nine parameters $d, t, c, qs, qd, b, sf, bw, t_l$ together to a vector of nine parameters

$$e = (d, t, c, qs, qd, b, sf, bw, t_l) \tag{7.1}$$

Let us call a specific vector e a *configuration*. There are two restrictions between the parameters. The number of dimensions d of the data space must be larger than or equal to the number qd of dimensions in which the query box is restricted. The number of indexed tuples must be larger or equal than the cardinality c of attributes. In the remaining part of this chapter only configurations in which the restrictions $qd \leq d$ and $c \leq t$ are considered.

For each parameter in e a set of values is defined. $E.\,g.$ for the blocksize b, let $B = \{4, 8, 16\}$. For the other parameters, value sets are defined similarly and denoted by capitalized letters. The set of all configurations is defined as:

$$E = \{(d, t, c, qs, qd, b, sf, bw, t_l) \quad\quad\quad\quad (7.2)$$
$$\in D \times Nt \times C \times Q_s \times Q_d \times B \times SF \times BW \times T_l | (qd \leq d) \wedge (c \leq t)\}$$

In the following experiments the parameters bw and t_l are kept constant for one set of parameter values. The set BW and the set T_l contains one value each.

7.3 Index Structures and Time Estimators

Our goal is to develop techniques for the comparison of index structures. This Section describes four for index structure models which are used for the comparison. We apply two tree-based index structures and the two bitmap index structures. We limit ourself firstly to the size of the index structure if the number of tuples and the cardinality of data which has to be indexed is given. Then we calculate the time which is needed to process range queries. For each index structure we define a function to estimate the time used for processing a given range query in a given configuration. This chapter applies $(s = 4)$ index structures. Therefore s different functions $t_i : E \rightarrow \mathbb{R}^+, i \in \{1, \cdots, s\}$ are defined to estimate the time for query processing:

$$t_i(e) = \quad \textbf{time for processing range query in configuration } e$$
$$\textbf{with index structure } i$$

Next we show how the functions t_i are calculated for the four index structures which we apply in this chapter.

7.3.1 Time Measures for Tree-Based Index Structures

First we apply a tree-based index structure without aggregated data in the inner nodes. We calculate the space needed for storing a tree-based index structure. Since there are much more leaf nodes than inner nodes (inner nodes occupy less than 2 % of the disk space in our experiments) we consider only leaf nodes. The number of leaf nodes is the same for structures that use aggregated data and for structures that omit materialized aggregates in the inner nodes. The space s_{data} (in Byte) needed by one entry of a leaf node depends on the cardinality of the attribute c_j and the dimensionality d of the data. In addition, a pointer ($Tuple\ IDendtifier = 4$ Bytes) to the data itself is stored:

$$s_{data} = \frac{\sum_{j=1}^{d} \lceil \log_2 c_j \rceil}{8} + \underbrace{4}_{tid} \quad\quad\quad\quad (7.3)$$

The maximum fanout of data pages or leaf pages depends on the chosen blocksize b and on the size of the data entries s_{data}. The greater the blocksize, the more data entries are stored on each block. This maximum number of entries B_{leaf} per block is given by:

$$B_{leaf} = \left\lfloor \frac{b * 1024}{s_{data}} \right\rfloor \tag{7.4}$$

We define the number of data nodes n (leaf nodes) necessary to store all data entries as the quotient of the number of tuples t that are indexed and the number of data entries B_{leaf} fitting into one block:

$$n = \left\lceil \frac{t}{B_{leaf}} \right\rceil \tag{7.5}$$

Here we assume that all nodes are filled with the maximum fanout. This is achieved if a bottom-up structure like the STR-tree [Leutenegger et al., 1997] or packed R-tree [Roussopoulos and Leifker, 1985] is used. Therefore, for other structures like the R^*-tree B_{leaf} has to be set to the average number of entries per leaf node. For the R^*-tree this is approximately 70 % of the maximum fanout.

We assume that blocks are not stored on the disk in a specific ordering. Each page access to disk requires one random access. The number of necessary disk accesses can be computed by measures presented in Chapter 6. The time estimation $t_1 : E \to \mathbb{R}$ for the tree *without* aggregated data is the expected number of necessary page accesses $Inter(q)$ multiplied by the time needed for one random access t_r. The calculation of the form of a range query q depends on parameters qs and qd of configuration e as presented on page 92. Given this vector q and the other parameters of the tree-based index structure we define the time from the given configuration e as the product of expected number of disk accesses times random access time:

$$t_1(e) = Inter(q) * t_r \tag{7.6}$$

Chapter 5 described the idea of aggregated data in the inner nodes of an index structure in detail. If aggregated data is used, there is no access necessary to rectangles completely contained in the query box. $Border(q)$ is the number of leaf nodes which have to be accessed when *aggregated* data is used. Then the expected time $t_2(e)$ for the tree-based structure with use of aggregated data is the product of the number of accessed pages and the time for a random block access t_r:

$$t_2(e) = Border(q) * t_r \tag{7.7}$$

We use the two measures t_1 and t_2 to estimate the time for a given configuration to process a query with tree structures. There are approaches in which blocks are stored in some ordering (e. g. Hilbert-curve or the Z-curve).

For few dimensions (two to three) this reduces the number of random block accesses because blocks are read sequentially. However, this effect is only effective for few dimensions and for a high number of dimensions this effect can be neglected.

7.3.2 Time Measures for Bitmap Indexing Techniques

This section investigates bitmap indexing techniques. Bitmaps indexes perform differently from tree-based indexing techniques. Details of bitmap indexing techniques are presented in Section 3.6. This chapter uses multi-component equality encoded bitmap indexes and multi-component range based encoded bitmap indexes. For simplicity, we use the terms equality encoded and range encoded here.

Here, we concentrate on *time optimal bitmap indexes under a given space constraint* [Chan and Ioannidis, 1998]. To compare bitmap index structures with tree structures, we assume that the space constraint depends on the space the tree structure needs multiplied by scale factor sf. First the size of each bitmap vector (*e. g.* size of B_1 in Figure 3.10 on page 28) is determined. The number of blocks necessary for storing one bitmap vector depends on the number of tuples t and on the blocksize b:

$$v = \left\lceil \frac{t}{8 * 1024 * b} \right\rceil \tag{7.8}$$

This model assumes that the size of the space which is occupied by bitmap vectors is proportional to the space needed by tree structures. Let m denote the number of bitmap vectors that are stored by the system. This value of m depends on the blocks allocated by the tree structure and a scale factor sf, which is one of our input parameters:

$$m = \left\lfloor \frac{n * sf}{v} \right\rfloor \tag{7.9}$$

The space constraint m gives the maximum number of bitmap vectors for all dimensions together. We split the *global* m into separate m_j for each dimension $j = 1, 2, \cdots, d$ with $\sum_{j=1}^{d} m_j \leq m$ weighted by the cardinality c_j:

$$m_j = \left\lfloor m \frac{\log c_j}{\sum_{j=1}^{d} \log c_j} \right\rfloor \tag{7.10}$$

The m_j's are used to calculate the base of the encoded bitmap indexes in each dimension. For equality and range encoded bitmap indexing techniques we get different structures. Therefore, we have to distinguish between the bases for the two distinct bitmap indexing techniques. Having the m_j and

c_j at hand, we calculate the bases of the equality encoded bitmap index as shown in Figure 3.12 on page 31.

Estimator B_{equal} in Equation 3.9 on page 33 calculates the number of bitmap vectors which are read when processing a range query with equality encoded bitmap indexes. The first block access is a random block access while the other block accesses are read sequentially. The time for processing the range query is calculated by:

$$t_3(e) = (t_r + (v - 1)t_s) * B_{equal} \qquad (7.11)$$

Figure 3.15 on page 33 shows the calculation of the base of the bitmap index with given m_j for range encoded bitmap indexes. Equation 3.17 on page 33 defines for a given base the number of bitmap indexes which are read. Given the estimator for the range encoded bitmap vectors as B_{range}, we calculate the time needed for the range encoded bitmap index as:

$$t_4(e) = (t_r + (v - 1)t_s) * B_{range} \qquad (7.12)$$

This section defined four functions t_1, t_2, t_3, and t_4 to calculate the time for processing a configuration e with an index structure. In Table 7.1 the four functions are summarized. The functions t_1 and t_2 provide functions of the expected time for processing range queries using trees. The functions t_3 and t_4 define the expected time for access the data with bitmap indexing techniques.

Table 7.1. Functions to estimate the processing time using various index structures

Function	Index Structure
t_1	R-tree without aggregated data
t_2	R-tree with aggregated data
t_3	Equality encoded bitmap index
t_4	Range encoded bitmap index

7.4 Classification Trees

This section applies classification trees to get information about the most important parameters which influence the performance of index structures. Classification trees are important tools in detecting latent structures in data [Venables and Ripley, 1994]. Classification trees use a set of objects or tuples, a set of one or more classification variables, and one response variable [Breimann et al., 1984]. A classification tree can be reviewed as a hierarchical collection of rules: For example, for tuple $a \in O$ the rule set may look like:

if $(x \leq 3)$ and $(y \leq 5)$ then a belongs most likely to group A
if $(x \leq 3)$ and $(y > 5)$ then a belongs most likely to group B
if $(x > 3)$ then a belongs most likely to group C

Fig. 7.1. Simple example of a classification tree

In this example are x and y the classification variables, a is a tuple or data item and the response variable can take values in $O = \{A, B, C\}$. Figure 7.1 displays the rules in the form of a binary tree. When constructing a classification tree there are two contradicting objectives. First, a classification tree should be rather small in terms of terminal nodes. This objective yields to too general trees. The extreme case is a generated tree consisting of only one terminal node. The second objective is to classify as many data items correct as possible. This objective leads to rather large trees. In the extreme case a tree has one different terminal node for each data item. Such extreme classification trees are rather useless. The main goal is to find an appropriate tradeoff between the size of the tree and its accuracy measured as a misclassification rate.

7.4.1 Applied Methods

This section describes how classification trees are applied for comparing index structures. For each configuration $e \in E$, the expected times are computed for processing the specified query for s tree structures. This is done by applying the functions $t_i : E \rightarrow \mathbb{R}$ defined in Section 7.3. The best (fastest) index of all structures is selected by a function $s_{min} : E \rightarrow \{1, \cdots, s\}$ which is defined as:

$$s_{min}(e) = \min\{i \in \{1, \cdots, s\} | t_i(e) \leq t_j(e) \quad \forall j \in \{1, \cdots, s\}\} \qquad (7.13)$$

For each configuration $e \in E$, function $s_{min} : E \rightarrow \{1, \cdots, s\}$ selects the fastest index structure. The input set for the generation of the classification tree consists of ten-dimensional vectors. The first nine values are the parameters defined by e. The last value is the response variable and corresponds to the index of the fastest index structure. Formally we define this set G for constructing the classification tree as:

$$G = \{(\underbrace{d, t, c, qs, qd, b, sf, bw, t_l}_{e}, s_{min}(e)) | e \in E\}$$

Table 7.2 shows an example of the set G. This set G is the input for the statistical software package S-Plus.

Table 7.2. Set G for generation classification tree

d	t	c	qs	dq	b	sf	bw	t_l	$s_{min(e)}$
1	10^6	3	10^{-7}	1	4	1	60	6	0
1	10^6	3	10^{-7}	1	4	2	60	6	0
1	10^6	3	10^{-7}	1	4	3	60	6	0
1	10^6	3	10^{-7}	1	8	1	60	6	0
1	10^6	3	10^{-7}	1	8	2	60	6	0
1	10^6	3	10^{-7}	1	8	3	60	6	0
$\vdots$	$\vdots$	$\vdots$	$\vdots$	$\vdots$	$\vdots$	$\vdots$	$\vdots$	$\vdots$	$\vdots$

7.4.2 Value Sets of Parameters

Table 7.3 shows the different experimental parameter sets. Altogether there are 42,336 cases considered for building a classification tree. This are fewer cases than for the aggregation technique presented in Table 7.4 because the software package S-Plus cannot handle such a large number of cases in a reasonable time.

We fix some parameters before running the software. The minimum number of elements of a node of a classification tree before the node is split is set to minsize=10. The minimum number of elements per node after a split is set to mincut=5.

Table 7.3. Parameter sets for experiments

Name	Variable name	Set name	Set of different values
Dimensions	d	D	$\{1, 2, 3, 4, 5, 6, 7\}$
Tuples	t	N_t	$\{10^6, 10^7, 10^8, 10^9\}$
Cardinality	c	C	$\{3, 10, 100, 10^3, 10^4, 10^5, 10^6\}$
Query box size	qs	Q_s	$\{10^{-7}, 10^{-6}, \cdots, 10^{-2}\}$
Query box dimensions	qd	Q_d	$\{1, 2, 3, 4, 5, 6, 7\}$
Block size [KB]	b	B	$\{4, 8, 16\}$
Scale factor	sf	SF	$\{1, 2, 3\}$
Bandwidth	bw	BW	today (2000): 11 MB/sec, in 5 years: 60 MB/sec
Latency time	t_l	T_l	today (2000): 6 ms, in 5 years: 4 ms

7.4.3 Results

The number of misclassified data items depends on the size of the tree. The more leaf nodes the tree consists of, the more data items are classified correctly. The smaller the tree is, the more data items are misclassified. Figure 7.2 shows the tradeoff between the number of misclassified data items and the size of the tree in number of leaf nodes. The x-axis shows the number of leaf nodes and the y-axis the number of misclassified data items. For 45 to 60 terminal nodes 6209 data items or 14.6 % of all data items are misclassified. If the tree is pruned to 32 leaf nodes, the misclassification rate increases to 16 % and for a tree with only 20 terminal nodes the misclassification rate is about 20.6 %.

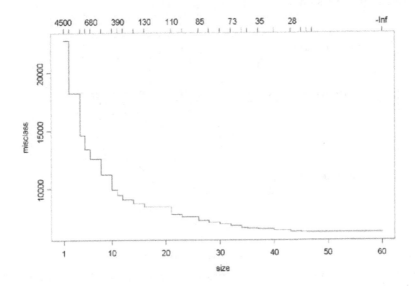

Fig. 7.2. Size of tree vs. misclassification of cases

In Figure 7.3 the generated classification tree with 20 leaf nodes is plotted. The 19 inner nodes guide the path to the leaf nodes. From this type of tree we extract two kinds of knowledge.

1. Rules: For this experimental setup we get 20 rules. We pick out the following rule for example:

If $sf > 1$ and $q_s > 10^{-4}$ and $d \leq 1 \Rightarrow R_a^*$-tree $\odot$

2. Importance of parameters: If a specific case $e \in E$ satisfies the precondition $(sf > 1$ and $q_s > 10^{-4}$ and $d \leq 1)$, the R_a^*-tree is the fastest structure.

These transactions have four properties: *A*tomicity, *C*onsistency, *I*solation, and *D*urability. They are abbreviated as ACID [Härder and Reuter, 1983] . Such applications are called On-Line Transaction Processing (OLTP) applications. Figure 2.1 shows an architecture with two OLTP applications accessing their databases. Graefe gives a general survey on query processing for these kinds of systems [Graefe, 1993].

Once the transaction-oriented data is stored in a database, a Decision Support System (DSS) is often built to create reports by grouping and summarizing data stored in the operational databases. There are various names for these kinds of systems; for instance, reporting tools, Management Information Systems (MIS), or executive information systems [Hannig, 1996]. In contrast to OLTP applications which read/write data from the operational databases, a DSS only reads data to get new information from the data sources. Figure 2.1 shows a DSS at the right side.

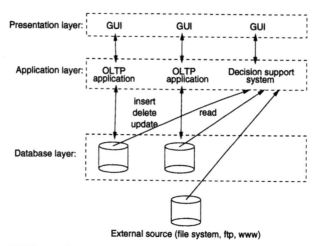

Fig. 2.1. OLTP application and information system based on operational database(s)

A benefit of this approach is that only the operational databases have to be created and maintained. A common set of metadata is used for both the operational system and the added-on DSS. The administration overhead for the DSS is rather small. However, there are significant disadvantages when the DSS and the transaction oriented application software share the same databases. The DSS can only use the actual data that is stored in the operational database. Therefore, historic analysis are usually not possible due to update or delete operations which changed the *historic* data. The operational database is optimized for transaction processes in a multi-user mode. This includes locking operations which do not support a scan of large sets of tuples

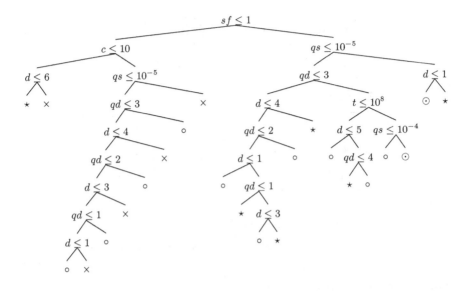

Fig. 7.4. Classification tree for year 2005 data

Figure 7.4 shows a classification tree which is generated with data for disks assumed to be available in five years. One interesting result of this tree is the fact that in more than two-third of all inner nodes the variables for the number of dimensions d or the variable for the query box dimensions qd occurs. In five years the variables d and qd influence the relative performance of the structures more than other parameters. Therefore, these parameters have to be carefully investigated.

Classification trees have one drawback. The input for the classification algorithm is the information which index structure is the fastest for a certain configuration. There is no information about the distance between the best solution and its competitors.

7.5 Statistics in Two Dimensions

This section describes an aggregation technique for comparing different index structures by keeping two parameters fixed [Jürgens and Lenz, 1999b].

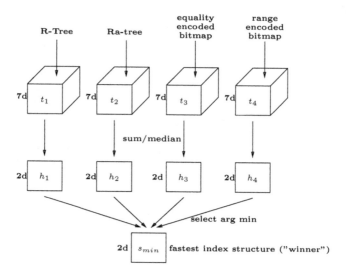

Fig. 7.5. Sum aggregation technique

Having defined the s functions from Section 7.3, the technique works in the following way: The two parameters bw and t_l are selected for one experiment. We create for each structure a seven-dimensional cube using the above defined functions t_i. Each cell of the seven-dimensional data cube stores the expected time for processing a range query for a given configuration. The seven-dimensional data is mapped to two-dimensional data by using statistical aggregation functions. Aggregation functions like *sum*, *min*, *max*, *count*, and *median* can be used as a measure of 'location' or 'mean' behaviour of an index structure. Next, we describe the *sum*, *median*, and *count* aggregation in detail.

7.5.1 Sum Aggregation

Figure 7.5 sketches how the sum aggregation is implemented. From each of the s different seven-dimensional data cubes, we generate a two-dimensional data cube by applying the aggregation function *sum*. Two dimensions are preselected into which we aggregate the data. Assume that the number of dimensions d and blocksize b are selected and that they are kept fixed. The aggregation is done by functions h_i, $i \in \{1, \cdots, s\}$ as follows:

$$h_i(d', b') = \sum_{(e \in E) \wedge (d=d') \wedge (b=b')} \underbrace{t_i(d, t, c, qs, qd, b, sf, bw, t_l)}_{e} \forall (d', b') \in D \times B$$

$$(7.14)$$

The *sum* function is proportional to the average case, because the number of cases is constant for all index structures. From the s two-dimensional data cubes, a two-dimensional cube is computed. Each cell of the resulting two-dimensional cube is computed by applying the function $s_{min} : D \times B \rightarrow \{1, \cdots, s\}$. The function s_{min} selects the index of the structure with the smallest value (shortest processing time). Function s_{min} is defined as:

$$s_{min}(d', b') = \min\{i \in \{1, \cdots, s\} | h_i(d', b') \le h_j(d', b') \; \forall j \in \{1, \cdots, s\}\}$$
$$\forall (d', b') \in D \times B \tag{7.15}$$

Functions like min or max can be used similarly as the sum function in Equation 7.14. An optimistic user may use the min function. A decision based on the min function assumes always the best case. A pessimistic user applies the max function.

7.5.2 Median Aggregation

The median aggregation method is similar to the sum aggregation method. The main difference is the definition of function h_i in Equation 7.14. Instead of calculating the sum of all values the $median$ as a less sensitive statistic (cf. [Huber, 1981]) is selected:

$$h_i(d', b') = \text{Median}\{t_i(\underbrace{d, t, c, qs, qd, b, sf, bw, t_l}_{e}) | e \in E \wedge (d = d') \wedge (b = b')\}$$
$$\forall (d', b') \in D \times B$$

The second part of the aggregation methods works similar to the sum aggregation.

7.5.3 Count Aggregation

A third aggregation technique is the count aggregation. This technique is implemented differently from the two previously described approaches. Figure 7.6 sketches the count aggregation technique. The count aggregation generates from s seven-dimensional data cubes one seven-dimensional data cube by selecting the index of the cube with the minimum value. Function s_{min} implements this selection:

$$s_{min}(e) = \min\{i | t_i(e) \le t_j(e) \; \forall j \in \{1, \cdots, s\}\} \tag{7.16}$$

From this seven dimensional cube one two-dimensional cube is generated by selecting the most frequent value for each subset.

$$h_i(d', b') = \text{mostFrequent}\{s_{min}(e) | e \in E \wedge e \in E \wedge d' = d \wedge b' = b\} \tag{7.17}$$

The count aggregation is less sensitive against extreme values, because all configurations are weighted equally.

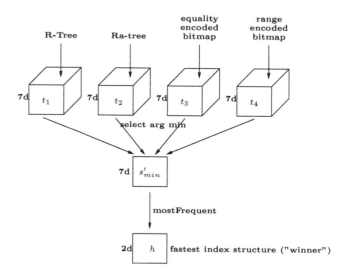

Fig. 7.6. Count aggregation technique

7.5.4 Results

This section presents results of experiments applying the aggregation technique. The results of the median aggregation method and count aggregation method are similar to the *sum* aggregation method. Therefore, we present only results of sum aggregation.

In the experiments the bandwidth bw and the latency time t_l are set to fixed values. We vary the remaining seven parameters and all possible combinations of the sets in Table 7.4 (under the constraint $(qd \leq d) \wedge (c \leq t)$). This yields in 617,760 different combinations for each index structure. For each of these combinations the four functions t_i are evaluated. Then we apply the aggregation as described previously. There are $\frac{n(n-1)}{2} = 21$ different possibilities, on how to aggregate the seven-dimensional data into two-dimensional data. All two-dimensional results are presented here for today's disk systems and for disk system expected in five years. The parameters for the disk are the parameters of a Seagate Cheetah 18. The latency time t_l is set to 6 ms and the bandwidth bw is set to 11 MB/sec [Patterson and Keeton, 1998]. Some of the results are discussed next.

On the very left of the topmost line of pictures in Figure 7.7 the data is aggregated according to the number of dimensions and the scale factor. This graph shows that for more than three dimensions the bitmap indexes perform faster than the tree-based index structures. For two or less dimensions the tree structures with aggregated data are best.

The right most picture in the third row in Figure 7.7 compares the cardinality c and the number of query box dimensions qd. This picture shows that

Table 7.4. Parameter sets for experiments

Name	Variable name	Set name	Set of different values
Dimensions	d	D	$\{1, 2, 3, 4, 5, 6, 7, 8, 9\}$
Tuples	t	N_t	$\{10^6, 3*10^6, 10^7, \cdots, 3*10^{10}\}$
Cardinality	c	C	$\{3, 10, 100, 10^3, 10^4, 10^5, 10^6, 10^7\}$
Query box size	qs	Q_s	$\{10^{-8}, 3*10^{-8}, 10^{-7}, \cdots, 10^{-3}\}$
Query box dimensions	qd	Q_d	$\{1, 2, 3, 4, 5, 6, 7, 8, 9\}$
Blocksize [KB]	b	B	$\{2, 4, 8, 16\}$
Scale factor	sf	SF	$\{1, 2, 3, 4\}$
Bandwidth	bw	BW	today (2000): 11 MB/sec, in 5 years: 60 MB/sec
Latency time	t_l	T_l	today (2000): 6 ms, in 5 years: 4 ms

for queries which are restricted in more than four dimensions the tree-based index structures with aggregated data are well suited. If queries are restricted in only two to three dimensions, bitmap indexes are superior.

The very left picture in the fifth row in Figure 7.7 compares the number of dimensions d and the attribute cardinality c. It can be seen that for more than 2 to 3 dimensions the bitmaps are better than the tree structures.

In Figure 7.8 the third row compares the query box size qs and the number of query box dimensions qd. If only one or two attributes occur in the range query, the bitmap indexes outperform the trees. If the query box is very small (nearly a point query) aggregated data in inner nodes of the trees cannot be used and the tree without aggregated data works most efficiently for $qd > 2$. If the query box size is increased, the tree with aggregated data becomes superior. However, for very large query boxes, the range encoded bitmap works best.

Figure 7.9 and Figure 7.10 show the results of the same experiments as shown in Figure 7.7 and Figure 7.8, but the bandwidth bw and the latency time t_l are changed. In the area of new computer technology it is very difficult and risky to make any predictions for the future. If we assume that the bandwidth bw increases by 40 % each year and the latency time t_l is decreasing by only 8 % per year (like bw and t_l did during the last years [Bitton and Gray, 1998], [Patterson and Keeton, 1998]), the models we presented here can be used to predict the performance of index structures with new disk technology. Here, we extrapolate this trend, present results for disk systems expected to be available in five years and compare them with results of today's disk systems.

Figure 7.9 and Figure 7.10 show that the bitmaps gain advantages over the tree-based indexing techniques with the use of future disk technology. In the next years, in many more cases range encoded bitmap indexes are

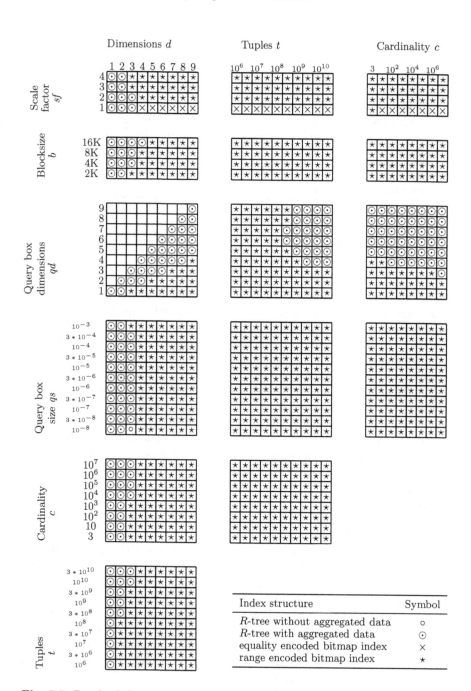

Fig. 7.7. Results I: Sum aggregation technique (year 2000)

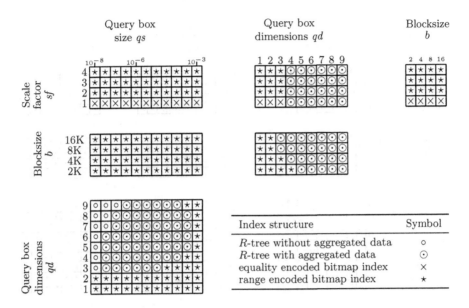

Fig. 7.8. Results II: Sum aggregation technique (year 2000)

faster than its competitors than today. This trend becomes evident if the number of dimensions is considered. Comparing the first column of pictures in Figure 7.7 with the first column of pictures in Figure 7.9 shows that with 2000s disk drives the bitmap are better than the trees for at least three dimensions. With the expected disk technology of 2005 the bitmaps are in many cases better than tree-based index structures.

Bitmaps are gaining advantages in comparison to trees, because they read large blocks of data. Trees access only small blocks and suffer from long latency times t_l.

7.6 Summary

For data warehouses fast access to large sets of data is crucial. Index structures support query processing. Many parameters influence the performance of index structures. Here we concentrate on a set of nine parameters. We present two techniques to compare different index structures for the use in a data warehouses. Classification trees generate rules to evaluate which index structure is suited best for a specific experimental setup. Further results are information about what parameters influence the performance of index structures most. One evidence is, that the chosen blocksize for a database is only of limited influence, but the scale factor sf is very important, because it is first selected feature in the induced classification trees. Statistical function and aggregation methods show in which cases specific index structures

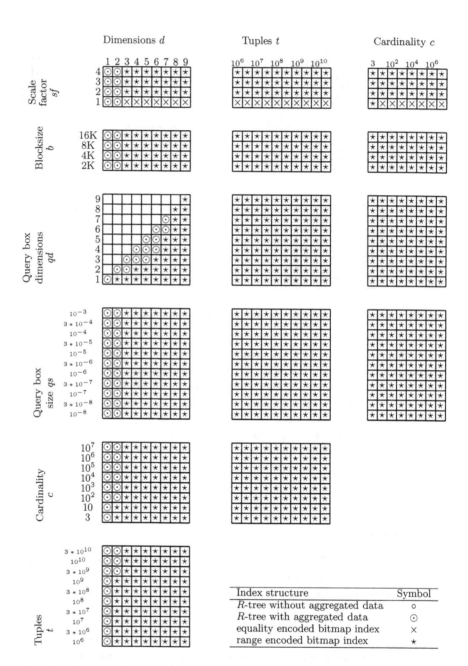

Fig. 7.9. Results III: Sum aggregation technique (year 2005)

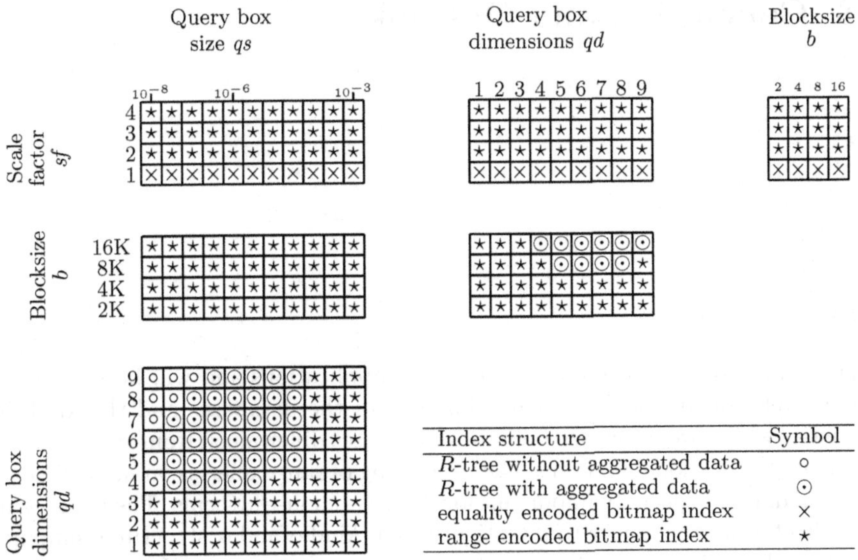

Index structure	Symbol
R-tree without aggregated data	○
R-tree with aggregated data	⊙
equality encoded bitmap index	×
range encoded bitmap index	⋆

Fig. 7.10. Results IV: Sum aggregation technique (year 2005)

outperform other index structures. In addition, we show that due to changes in disk technology, bitmap indexing techniques will gain advantages over the traditional tree-based index structures in the future.

8 Conclusion and Outlook

Data warehouses are important database applications and will become even more relevant in the next years. The size of the databases and the kind of queries which are processed on data warehouses differ much from transaction-oriented operational systems. The processing of range queries on multidimensional data is especially important for data warehouse systems. The main goal of this thesis is therefore to investigate what kind of index structures support efficiently typical queries in a data warehouse environment. For data warehouse applications multidimensional tree-based index structures and bitmap indexes are the most promising structures. The R^*-tree is well known for its robustness. Variants of the standard bitmap indexing techniques overcome the problem of space inefficiency and the problem of weak support for range queries.

In read-mostly environments, fast query processing is more important than short update phases. The better the data is clustered onto pages, the faster the queries are processed. This thesis described one approach for finding *optimal* index structures by transforming the problem of clustering data into a mixed integer problem (MIP). This approach guarantees finding optimal solutions. Software packages cplex and MOPS can solve the defined MIP numerically. These clusterings are marginally better than the solutions generated by R^*-trees. Due to its time complexity the MIP approach can only be used for very small data sets to evaluate the quality of heuristics. For real size data sets the MIP approach is not applicable. The problem of finding an optimal index structure in polynomial time remains an open research question.

Typical queries in data warehouse applications compute aggregated data from large sets of tuples. For processing this kind of queries, we *improved* tree-based index structures by an extension where materialized aggregated data is stored in the inner nodes. This thesis investigated what kind of data can be calculated and materialized inside the index structure. We showed how to change the insert and query algorithms to maintain and use the aggregated data inside the inner nodes. We presented an upper bound to estimate the space overhead for aggregated materialized data. Experiments showed that

M. Juergens: Index Structures for Data Warehouses, LNCS 1859, pp. 113-115, 2002.
© Springer-Verlag Berlin Heidelberg 2002

the extension decreases significantly the number of necessary disk accesses for processing range queries on aggregated data.

To *estimate* the performance of index structures analytically, we compared performance models for tree-based structures. The GRID model, SUM model, and FRACTAL model are known from literature. The GRID and SUM model assume uniformly distributed data. The FRACTAL model uses the ratio between the part of data space which is covered by the real data and and the whole data space. We extended the models to include aggregated data in the inner nodes of the index structure. Then, we developed the new PISA model (Performance of Index Structures with and without Aggregated data). The main advantage of PISA model compared to the previous existing models is that PISA considers the actual distribution of data and the distribution of queries. In this thesis, we adapted PISA model to uniform, skewed, and normal distributions of data and queries. Experiments showed that the PISA model is more accurate than the other models in most cases.

This thesis provided techniques to *compare* index structures for data warehouses. The performance of index structures depends on different parameters. We described nine parameters which influence query processing time. We defined parameterized performance measures to calculate the expected time needed to execute specified queries. We varied the parameters and generate sets of experimental cases. We generated structured information in form of classification trees from data sets. Classification trees provided concrete rules in which situation which index structure performs best. In addition, classification trees showed which parameters influence the performance of the index structure most. One result of the experiments is that the blocksize does not influence the relative performance between the structures. To see how the performance of index structure depend on certain parameters, an aggregation method condenses high-dimensional data into two-dimensional data. The resulting figures show that bitmap indexes are faster than tree based index structures for at least four dimensions. For less than three dimensions tree structures perform better. Another interesting result is that if the trend of evolving disk technology continues with the same speed as it did in the last years, the bitmap indexes techniques will get more efficient relative to the tree structure with the time. Bitmap indexes profit from the fact that the time gap between a random block access and a sequential block access is getting greater with every new generation of disk technology.

There are many open research questions in this field of index structures for data warehouses. One of the rather theoretically interesting questions is to find an *optimal* index structure in polynomial time.

We believe that storing aggregated data in the inner nodes of a tree structure is sufficiently investigated in this thesis. The presented performance models to estimate the number of disk accesses can be evaluated with more data sets in different experiments. However, techniques to extend the model to different kinds of data and/or to consider the other levels of a tree are presented in this thesis.

An important starting point for research about index structures are bitmap indexing techniques. Bitmap indexes are well suited for high dimensional data with a small number of different values. The bitmap indexes use hardware efficiently because bitmaps indexes read large blocks of data and perform Boolean operations on these large blocks of bits. Therefore, bitmap indexes exhibit advantages over tree-based indexing techniques for many data warehouse applications. Since they profit from new disk technology more than tree-based indexing methods and they are not investigated in such detail as the tree-based index structures are, we believe that there is a great potential for developing new indexing structures based on bitmaps.

A List of Symbols

a	length of interval A	page 72
A	set of all index entries	page 18
a_j	name of jth attribute	page 18
A_j	set of extensions of attribute a_j	page 18
b	blocksize	page 16
B	set of distinct blocksizes	page 95
B_{dir}	maximum fanout of directory node	page 24
b_{dir}	minimum fanout of directory node	page 24
B_{equal}	expected number of bitmap vectors which are read for an equality encoded bitmap index for processing a range query	page 31
b_j	number of bitmap vectors in j's dimension	page 30
b_{ji}	the ith bitmap vector on the jth attribute	page 30
B_{leaf}	maximum fanout of leaf node	page 24
b_{leaf}	minimum fanout of leaf node	page 24
B_{range}	expected number of bitmap vectors which are read for a range encoded bitmap index for processing a range query	page 33

M. Juergens: Index Structures for Data Warehouses, LNCS 1859, pp. 117-122, 2002.
© Springer-Verlag Berlin Heidelberg 2002

$Border(q)$	number of blocks that have to be accessed when an R_a^*-tree is used: $Inter(q) - Contain(q)$	page 46
bw	bandwith	page 94
BW	set of distinct bandwidths	page 94
c	cardinality of data space	page 92
C	set of distinct cardinalities of data space	page 95
c_j	cardinality of data space in jth dimension	page 18
$Contain(q)$	number of leaf nodes contained in query box q	page 46
cp	child pointer	page 23
d	number of dimensions	page 18
D	set of distinct number of dimensions	page 95
$d_a(x)$	density function of position of interval A	page 73
$d_b(y)$	density function of position of interval B	page 73
d_f	fractal dimension	page 69
$data_{entry}$	entry of a data node	page 48
dir_{entry}	entry of a directory node	page 47
DW	data warehouse	page 7
e	configuration vector $(d, t, c, qs, qd, b, sf, bw, t_l)$	page 94
E	set of all configurations: $\{(d, t, c, qs, qd, b, sf, bw, t_l)\| (d, t, c, qs, qd, b, sf, bw, t_l) \in D \times N_t \times C \times Q_s \times Q_d \times B \times SF \times BW \times T_l, (qd \le d) \wedge (c \le t)\}$	page 95

$f(u,v)$	additional space when switching from fanout of u to fanout of v	page 53
$f(x,y)$	characteristic function to decide if two intervals intersect	page 73
$g(x,y)$	characteristic function to decide if one intervals is contained in the other	page 74
G	input set for creation of classification tree	page 99
h	height of tree	page 52
$h_1(a,b)$	PISA model: probability that A intersects B	page 73
$h_2(a,b)$	PISA model: probability that A contains B	page 74
i	index	
I	multi dimensional interval	page 18
$Inter(q)$	number of leafs intersecting query box q	page 46
j	index on the number of dimensions	
k	number of classes of the user defined density function	page 75
K	upper bound for additional space	page 53
l_{ik}	lower border of block i in dimension k	page 36
m	total number of bitmap vectors that are stored by an bitmap index in all dimensions	page 97
m_j	number of bitmap vectors that are stored by an bitmap index in the jth dimension	page 30
M	boxes for fractal dimension model	page 69
M_f	boxes filled for fractal dimension model	page 69

n	number of leaf nodes	page 36
N	set $\{1, \cdots, n\}$	page 69
n_i	number of nodes on level i	
	n_0: number of leaf nodes	
	n_1: number of inner nodes on level 1	
	n_h: number of root nodes ($n_h = 1$)	
n_u	number of leaf nodes of structure with fanout u	page 53
n_v	number of leaf nodes of structure with fanout v	page 53
N_t	set with distinct number of tuples	page 95
O	$O_1 \times \cdots \times O_d = \{0, \cdots, c_1 - 1\} \times \cdots \times \{0, \cdots, c_d - 1\}$	page 18
O_j	$\{0, \cdots, c_j - 1\}$	page 18
OP	set of operations	page 7
P	set of d-dimensional points (tuples)	page 36
p_i	SUM model: probability that rectangle i intersects query box q	page 66
q	vector with size of query box $q = (q_1, \cdots, q_d)$ (length in each dimension)	page 19
q_j	length of query box in jth dimension	page 19
qd	query box dimensions	page 92
Q_d	set with distinct query box dimensions	page 95
qs	query box size	page 92
Q_s	set of distinct query box sizes	page 95

R	Relation $R(a_1, \cdots, a_n, s)$	page 10
r_{ij}	size of leaf node i in dimension j	page 66
$\tilde{r}$	average length of rectangle in SUM model and PISA model (1-case)	page 75
r'	average length of rectangle in FRACTAL model	page 70
$\overline{r}$	average length of rectangle in GRID model	page 65
s_{dir}	size of a directory entry	page 46
s_{min}	select the index of the structure with the minimum value	page 99
s	number of index structures which are compared	page 95
s_0	number of slice for approximation of PISA model	page 124
S	data space $[0, 1)^d$	page 64
sf	scale factor	page 93
SF	set with distinct scale factors	page 95
t	number of tuples	page 36
T	$\{1, \cdots, t\}$	page 36
tid	tuple identifier	page 18
t_r	time for random block access to secondary memory	page 17
t_s	time for sequential block access to secondary memory	page 17

B Approximation of PISA Model

The integral in Equation 6.14 on page 73 and the integral in Equation 6.17 on page 74 cannot be computed for every $d_a(x)$ and $d_b(y)$ analytically. For these cases we apply approximation methods to compute the integrals numerically. Appendix B presents approximation method for computing the integral in Equation 6.14. Equation 6.17 is approximated similarly. We present the computation of the integral over the gray shaded area in Figure B.1. Functions u and l describe this area:

$$u(x) = \begin{cases} x + a & : \quad 0 \le x < 1 - a - b \\ 1 - b & : \quad 1 - a - b \le x \le 1 - a \end{cases}$$

$$l(x) = \begin{cases} 0 & : \quad 0 \le x < b \\ x - b & : \quad b \le x \le 1 - a \end{cases}$$

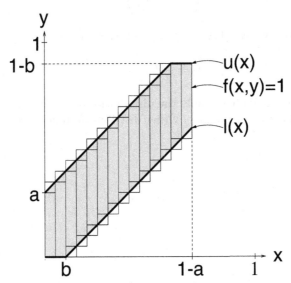

Fig. B.1. Approximation of the integral

M. Juergens: Index Structures for Data Warehouses, LNCS 1859, pp. 123-124, 2002.
© Springer-Verlag Berlin Heidelberg 2002

Figure B.1 shows the area divided in $s_0 = 14$ slices. In computations presented in this thesis the x-interval $[0, 1 - a)$ is divided in $s_0 = 200$ equidistant slices. Integrals over two rectangles are calculated for each interval. One sum of rectangles calculates an upper bound (U) of the real value and another sum of rectangles calculates a lower bound (L) of the real result:

$$U(a,b) \;=\; \sum_{x \in \{y \mid y = (1-a)\frac{i}{s_0} \wedge i \in \{0, \cdots, s_0 - 1\}\}} \left(\Phi_{\mu,\sigma} \left(x + \frac{1}{s_0}, u_{a,b} \left(x + \frac{1}{s_0} \right) \right) \right) \tag{B.1}$$

$$- \quad \Phi_{\mu,\sigma} \left(x, u_{a,b} \left(x + \frac{1}{s_0} \right) \right) \tag{B.2}$$

$$- \quad \Phi_{\mu,\sigma} \left(x + \frac{1}{s_0}, l_{a,b} \left(x + \frac{1}{s_0} \right) \right) \tag{B.3}$$

$$+ \quad \Phi_{\mu,\sigma} \left(x, l_{a,b} \left(x \right) \right)$$

$$L(a,b) \;=\; \sum_{x \in \{y \mid y \ (1-a)\frac{i}{s_0} \wedge i \in \{0, \cdots, s_0 - 1\}\}} \left(\Phi_{\mu,\sigma} \left(x + \frac{1}{s_0}, u_{a,b} \left(x \right) \right) \tag{B.4}$$

$$- \quad \Phi_{\mu,\sigma} \left(x, u_{a,b} \left(x \right) \right) \tag{B.5}$$

$$- \quad \Phi_{\mu,\sigma} \left(x + \frac{1}{s_0}, l_{a,b} \left(x + \frac{1}{s_0} \right) \right) \tag{B.6}$$

$$+ \quad \Phi_{\mu,\sigma} \left(x, l_{a,b} \left(x + \frac{1}{s_0} \right) \right)$$

The arithmetic average of these two sums is the approximation of the integral:

$$h_2(a,b) = \frac{1}{2}(U(a,b) + L(a,b)) \tag{B.7}$$

The equations shown here apply the distribution function $\Phi_{\mu,\sigma}(x)$ of normal distributed data as an example. Other distribution functions can be applied as well.

Bibliography

[Anahory and Murray, 1997] Anahory, S. and Murray, D. (1997). *Data Warehousing in the Real World.* Addison-Wesley, Essex.

[Arge, 1995] Arge, L. (1995). The buffer tree: A new technique for optimal I/O algorithms. In *International Workshop on Algorithms and Data Structures*, LNCS 1460, pages 334–345, Berlin/New York. Springer.

[Bayer, 1996] Bayer, R. (1996). The universal B-tree for multidimensional indexing. Technical Report TUM-I9637, Technische Universität München.

[Bayer and Markl, 1998] Bayer, R. and Markl, V. (1998). The UB-tree: Performance of multidimenisional range queries. Technical Report TUM-I9814, Technische Universität München.

[Bayer and McCreight, 1972] Bayer, R. and McCreight, E. (1972). Organization and maintenance of large ordered indexes. *Acta Informatica*, 1(3):173–189.

[Beckmann et al., 1990] Beckmann, N., Kriegel, H.-P., Schneider, R., and Seeger, B. (1990). The R*-tree: An efficient and robust access method for points and rectangles. In *Proceedings of the 1985 ACM SIGMOD International Conference on Management of Data*, pages 322–331, New York.

[Bentley, 1975] Bentley, J. L. (1975). Multidimensional binary search trees used for associative searching. *Communications of the ACM*, 18(9):509–517.

[Berchtold et al., 1996] Berchtold, S., Keim, D. A., and Kriegel, H.-P. (1996). The X-tree: An index structure for high-dimensional data. In *Proceedings of the 22nd International Conferencen on Very Large Databases (VLDB)*, pages 28–39.

[Bitton and Gray, 1998] Bitton, D. and Gray, J. (1998). The rebirth of database machines. Invited talk at the 24th International Conference on Very Large Data Bases (VLDB).

[Box and Muller, 1958] Box, G. E. P. and Muller, M. E. (1958). A note on the generation of random normal deviates. *Ann. Math. Stat.*, 29:610–611.

[Breimann et al., 1984] Breimann, L., Friedmann, J. H., Olshen, R. A., and Stone, C. J. (1984). *Classification and Regression Trees.* Wadsworth and Brooks/Cole, Monterey.

[Chan and Ioannidis, 1998] Chan, C.-Y. and Ioannidis, Y. E. (1998). Bitmap index design and evaluation. In *Proceedings of the International Conference on Management of Data*, pages 355 – 366.

[Chan and Ioannidis, 1999] Chan, C.-Y. and Ioannidis, Y. E. (1999). An efficient bitmap encoding scheme for selection queries. In *SIGMOD Conference 1999*, pages 215–226.

[Chaudhuri and Dayal, 1997] Chaudhuri, S. and Dayal, U. (1997). An overview of data warehousing and OLAP technology. *SIGMOD Record*, 26(1):65–74.

[Chen et al., 1998] Chen, L., Choubey, R., and Rundensteiner, E. A. (1998). Bulk-insertions into R-trees using the small-tree-large-tree approach. In *Proceedings of the 6th international symposium on Advances in geographic information systems*, pages 161–162.

M. Juergens: Index Structures for Data Warehouses, LNCS 1859, pp. 125–130, 2002.
© Springer-Verlag Berlin Heidelberg 2002

[Christiansen et al., 1998] Christiansen, A., Höding, M., Rautenstrauch, C., and Saake, G. (1998). *Oracle8 effizient einsetzen - Aufbau, Entwicklung, Verteilung und Betrieb leistungsfähiger Oracle8-Anwendungen*. Addison Wesley.

[Codd, 1994] Codd, E. F. (1994). Adding value to relational and legacy DBMS: The OLAP mandate. *Business Intelligence*.

[Faloutsos and Kamel, 1994] Faloutsos, C. and Kamel, I. (1994). Beyond uniformity and independence: Analysis of R- trees using the concept of fractal dimension. In *PODS '94. Proceedings of the Thirteenth ACM SIGACT-SIGMOD-SIGART Symposium on Principles of Database Systems*, volume 13, pages 4–13, New York. ACM Press.

[Finkel and Bentley, 1974] Finkel, R. A. and Bentley, J. L. (1974). Quad trees: a data structure for retrieval on composite keys. *Acta Informatica*, 4(1):1–9.

[Gaede and Günther, 1998] Gaede, V. and Günther, O. (1998). Multidimensional access methods. *ACM Computing Surveys*, 30(2):170–231.

[Garcia-Molina et al., 1999] Garcia-Molina, H., Ullman, J. D., and Widom, J. (1999). *Database Implementation*. Prentice Hall, Upper Saddle River, New Yersey.

[Graefe, 1993] Graefe, G. (1993). Query evaluation techniques for large databases. *ACM Computing Surveys*, 25(2):73–170.

[Gray et al., 1997] Gray, J., Chaudhuri, S., Bosworth, A., Layman, A., Reichart, D., and Venkatrao, M. (1997). Data cube: A relational aggregation operator generalizing group-by, cross-tab, and sub-totals. *Data Mining and Knowledge Discovery*, 1(1):29–53.

[Gray and Reuter, 1993] Gray, J. and Reuter, A. (1993). *Transaction Processing: Concepts and Techniques*. Morgan Kaufmann, San Mateo.

[Großer, 1997] Großer, P. (1997). Verwaltung relationaler Daten mit Hilfe einer mehrdimensionalen Indexstruktur. Master's thesis, Humboldt-Universität zu Berlin, Institut für Informatik.

[Günther, 1989] Günther, O. (1989). The design of the cell tree: An object-oriented index structure for geometric databases. In *Proceedings of the Fifth International Conference on Data Engineering (ICDE)*, pages 598–605. IEEE Computer Society.

[Günther et al., 1998] Günther, O., Oria, V., Picouet, P., Saglio, J.-M., and Scholl, M. (1998). Benchmarking spatial joins à la carte. In *Proceedings of the 10th International Conference on Scientific and Statistical Database Management, Proceedings*, pages 32–41, New York. IEEE Computer Society.

[Gupta et al., 1997] Gupta, H., Harinaryan, V., Rajaraman, A., and Ullman, J. D. (1997). Index selection for OLAP. In *Proceedings of the International Conference on Data Engineering (ICDE)*, pages 208–219.

[Gurret and Rigaux, 1998] Gurret, C. and Rigaux, P. (1998). An integrated platform for the evaluation of spatial query processing strategies. In *Proceedings of the 9th International Conference on Database and Expert Systems Applications (DEXA)*, LNCS 1460, pages 757–766. Springer.

[Guttman, 1984] Guttman, A. (1984). R-trees: A dynamic index structure for spatial searching. In *SIGMOD'84, Proceedings of Annual Meeting, Boston, Massachusetts*, pages 47–57. ACM Press, New York.

[Haas, 1999] Haas, P. J. (1999). Techniques for online exploration of large object-relational datasets. In *International Conference on Scientific and Statistical Database Management (SSDBM)*, pages 4–12. IEEE Computer Society.

[Hannig, 1996] Hannig, U. (1996). *Data Warehouse und Management Informations Systeme*. Schäffer-Poeschel, Stuttgart.

[Härder and Rahm, 1999] Härder, T. and Rahm, E. (1999). *Datenbanksysteme - Konzepte und Techniken der Implementierung*. Springer, Berlin, Heidelberg.

[Härder and Reuter, 1983] Härder, T. and Reuter, A. (1983). Principles of transaction-oriented database recovery. *Computing Surveys*, 15(4):287–317.

[Hellerstein et al., 1997a] Hellerstein, J. M., Haas, P. J., and Wang, H. J. (1997a). Online aggregation. In *SIGMOD 1997, Proceedings ACM SIGMOD International Conference on Management of Data*, pages 171–182. ACM Press, New York.

[Hellerstein et al., 1997b] Hellerstein, J. M., Koutsoupias, E., and Papadimitriou, C. H. (1997b). On the analysis of indexing schemes. In *Proceedings of the Sixteenth ACM SIGACT-SIGMOD-SIGART Symposium on Principles of Database Systems*, pages 249–256. ACM Press, New York.

[Hellerstein et al., 1995] Hellerstein, J. M., Naughton, J. F., and Pfeffer, A. (1995). Generalized search trees for database systems. In *Proceedings of 21th International Conference on Very Large Data Bases (VLDB)*, pages 562–573. Morgan Kaufmann.

[Ho et al., 1997] Ho, C.-T., Agrawal, R., Megiddo, N., and Srikant, R. (1997). Range queries in OLAP data cubes. In Peckham, J., editor, *SIGMOD 1997, Proceedings ACM SIGMOD International Conference on Management of Data*, pages 73–88. ACM Press, New York.

[Huber, 1981] Huber, P. J. (1981). *Robust Statistics*. Wiley, New York.

[Huyn, 1997] Huyn, N. (1997). Muliple-view self-mainenance in data warehousing environments. In *Proceedings of the 23rd International Conference on Very Large Databases (VLDB)*, pages 26–35. Morgan Kaufmann, San Francisco, CA.

[Ibbetson, 1963] Ibbetson, D. (1963). Collected algorithms. *Commun. Ass. Computing Mach.*, 6:616. Algorithm 209 Gauss.

[Informix, 1997] Informix (1997). Indexing for the enterprise data warehouse. White paper. Available at http://www.informix.com.

[Inmon, 1996] Inmon, W. H. (1996). *Building the Data Warehouse*. Wiley & Sons, New York.

[Inmon et al., 1997] Inmon, W. H., Welch, J. D., and Katherine, G. L. (1997). *Managing the Data Warehouse*. Wiley & Sons, New York.

[Jürgens and Lenz, 1998] Jürgens, M. and Lenz, H.-J. (1998). The R_a^*-tree: An improved R^*-tree with materialized data for supporting range queries on OLAP-data. In *Proceedings of the International Workshop on Data Warehouse Design and OLAP Technology (DWDOT98)*, pages 186–191. IEEE Computer Society Press.

[Jürgens and Lenz, 1999a] Jürgens, M. and Lenz, H.-J. (1999a). PISA: Performance models of index structures with and without aggregated data. In *Proceedings of the 8th International Conference on Statistical and Scientific Database Management (SSDBM)*, pages 78–87. IEEE Computer Society.

[Jürgens and Lenz, 1999b] Jürgens, M. and Lenz, H.-J. (1999b). Tree based indexes vs. bitmap indexes: A performance study. In *International Workshop on Design and Management of Data Warehouses, Heidelberg*, pages 78–87.

[Kamel and Faloutsos, 1993] Kamel, I. and Faloutsos, C. (1993). On packing R-trees. In *2nd International Conference on Information and Knowledge Mangement (CIKM)*, pages 490–499. ACM Press, New York.

[Kamel and Faloutsos, 1994] Kamel, I. and Faloutsos, C. (1994). Hilbert R-tree: An improved R-tree using fractals. In *Proceedings of the 20st International Conference on Very Large Data Bases (VLDB)*, pages 500–509.

[Karayama and Satoh, 1997] Karayama, N. and Satoh, S. (1997). The SR-tree: An index structure for high-dimensional nearest neighbour queries. In *Proceedings ACM SIGMOD International Conference on Management of Data*, pages 369–380.

[Kornacker, 1999] Kornacker, M. (1999). High-performance extensible indexing. In *Proceedings of the 25rd International Conference on Very Large Databaseses (VLDB)*, pages 699–708. Morgan Kaufmann, San Farnsisco, CA.

[Kornacker et al., 1997] Kornacker, M., Mohan, C., and Hellerstein, J. M. (1997). Concurrency and recovery in generalized search trees. In Peckham, J., editor, *SIGMOD 1997, Proceedings ACM SIGMOD International Conference on Management of Data*, pages 62–72. ACM Press, New York.

[Kornacker et al., 1998] Kornacker, M., Shah, M., and Hellerstein, J. M. (1998). amdb: an access method debugging tool. In *SIGMOD 1998, Proceedings ACM SIGMOD International Conference on Management of Data, June 2-4, 1998*, pages 570–571. ACM Press, New York.

[Kuan and Lewis, 1999] Kuan, J. and Lewis, P. (1999). A study on data point search for HG-trees. *SIGMOD Record*, 28(1):90–96.

[Labio et al., 1997] Labio, W. J., Quass, D., and Adelberg, B. (1997). Physical database design for data warehouses. In *Proceedings of the ICDE*, pages 277–288.

[Lamersdorf et al., 1996] Lamersdorf, W., Lenz, H.-J., and Rieger, B. (1996). *Data Warehousing, OLAP, Führungsinformationssysteme... Neue Entwicklungen des Informationsmanagements*. Congress VIII, ONLINE GmbH Kongresse und Messen für Technische Kommunikation, Velbert.

[Lee and Hammer, 1999] Lee, M. and Hammer, J. (1999). Speeding up warehouse physical desing using a randomized algorithm. In *Proceedings of the International Workshop on Design and Management of Data Warehouses (DMDW'99)*.

[Lehner et al., 1998] Lehner, W., Albrecht, J., and Wedekind, H. (1998). Normal forms for multidimensional databases. In *10th International Conference on Scientific and Statistical Database Management*, pages 63–72. IEEE Computer Society.

[Lenz, 1993] Lenz, H.-J. (1993). On the design of statistical databases, micro-, marcro- und meta-database modelling. In Faulbaum, F., editor, *Advances in Statistical Software 5*. Gustav Fischer, Stuttgart.

[Lenz and Jürgens, 1998] Lenz, H.-J. and Jürgens, M. (1998). Modeling and improving the performance of multidimensional indexstructures for range queries on OLAP data. Technical Report 1998/29, Fachbereich Wirtschaftswissenschaft der Freien Universität Berlin.

[Lenz and Shoshani, 1997] Lenz, H. J. and Shoshani, A. (1997). Summarizability in OLAP and statistical data bases. In *Proceedings of 9th International Conference on Statistical and Scientific Database Management*, pages 132–143. IEEE Computer Society Press.

[Leutenegger and Lopez, 1998] Leutenegger, S. T. and Lopez, M. A. (1998). The effect of buffering on the performance of R-trees. In *Proceedings of the 14th International Conference on Data Engineering (ICDE)*, pages 164–171. IEEE Computer Society Press.

[Leutenegger et al., 1997] Leutenegger, S. T., López, M. A., and Edgington, J. M. (1997). STR: A simple and efficient algorithm for R-tree packing. In *Proceedings of the 13th International Conference on Data Engineering (ICDE)*, pages 497–506, Los Alamitos, California. IEEE Computer Society Press.

[Markl, 1999] Markl, V. (1999). *MISTRAL: Processing Relational Queries using a Multidimensional Access Technique*. PhD thesis, Technische Universität München.

[Marques et al., 1998] Marques, P., Furtado, P., and Baumann, P. (1998). An efficient strategy for tiling muldidimensional OLAP data cubes. In *GI Workshop on Data Mining and Data Warehousing, Magdeburg*, pages 13–24.

[O'Neil and Quass, 1997] O'Neil, P. and Quass, D. (1997). Improved query performance with variant indexes. *SIGMOD Record (ACM Special Interest Group on Management of Data)*, 26(2):38–49.

[Pagel, 1995] Pagel, B.-U. (1995). *Analyse und Optimierung von Indexstrukturen in GeoDatenbanksysteme*. PhD thesis, Fernuniversität Hagen.

[Pagel et al., 1993] Pagel, B.-U., Six, H.-W., Toben, H., and Widmayer, P. (1993). Towards an analysis of range query performance in spatial data structures. In *Proceedings of the Twelfth ACM SIGACT-SIGMOD-SIGART Symposium on Principles of Database Systems*, pages 214–221. ACM Press, New York.

[Patterson and Keeton, 1998] Patterson, D. A. and Keeton, K. K. (1998). Hardware technology trends and database opportunities. invited talk at SIGMOD 1998 International Conference on Management of Data.

[Robinson, 1981] Robinson, J. T. (1981). The K-D-B-tree: A search structure for large multidimensional dynamic indexes. In *Prodings of the ACM SIGMOD*, pages 10–18.

[Rotem and Zhao, 1996] Rotem, D. and Zhao, J. L. (1996). Extendible arrays for statistical databases and OLAP applications. In *Proceedings of the 8th International Conference on Statistical and Scientific Database Management (SSDBM)*, pages 108–117. IEEE Computer Society.

[Roussopoulos and Leifker, 1985] Roussopoulos, N. and Leifker, D. (1985). Direct spatial search on pictorial databases using packed R-trees. In *ACM SIGMOD (International Conference on Management of Data)*, pages 17–31, Austin, Texas.

[Samet, 1989] Samet, H. (1989). *Applications of Spatial Data Structures*. Addison-Wesley, Reading, Massachusetts.

[Samet, 1990] Samet, H. (1990). *The Design and Analysis of Spatial Data Structures*. Addison-Wesley, Reading, Massachusetts.

[Sapia, 1999] Sapia, C. (1999). On modeling and predicting user behaviour in OLAP systems. In *Proceedings of the International Workshop on Design and Management of Data Warehouses (DMDW'99)*.

[Sarawagi, 1997] Sarawagi, S. (1997). Indexing OLAP data. *Data Engineering Bulletin*, 20(1):36–43.

[Schnitzer and Leutenegger, 1999] Schnitzer, B. and Leutenegger, S. T. (1999). Master-client R-trees: A new parallel R-tree architecture. In *International Conference on Scientific and Statistical Database Management (SSDBM)*, pages 68–77.

[Sellis et al., 1985] Sellis, T., Roussopoulos, N., and Faloutsos, C. (1985). The R^+-tree: A dynamic index for multi-dimensional objects. In *Proceedings of the 13th international Conference on Very Large Databases (VLDB)*, pages 507–518.

[Shoshani, 1997] Shoshani, A. (1997). OLAP and statistical databases: Similarities and differences. In *Proceedings of the 16th ACM SIGACT-SIGMOD-SIGART Symposium on Principles of Database Systems*, pages 185–196.

[Shukla et al., 1996] Shukla, A., Deshpande, P. M., Naughton, J. F., and Ramasamy, K. (1996). Storage estimation for multidimensional aggregates in the presence of hierarcies. In *Proceedings of the 22nd International Conference on Very Large Databases (VLDB)*, pages 522–531.

[Srivastava et al., 1989] Srivastava, J., Tan, J. S. E., and Lum, V. Y. (1989). TB-SAM: An access method for efficient processing of statistical queries. *IEEE Transactions on Knowledge and Data Engineering*, 1(4):414–423.

[Suhl, 1998] Suhl, U. H. (1998). Mathematical optimizing system. Further information is available at http://mops.wiwiss.fu-berlin.de.

[Sybase, 1997] Sybase (1997). Adaptive server IQ. White paper. availabe at http://www.sybase.com.

[Theodoridis and Sellis, 1996] Theodoridis, Y. and Sellis, T. K. (1996). A model for the prediction of R-tree performance. In *Proceedings of the Fifteenth ACM SIGACT-SIGMOD-SIGART Symposium on Principles of Database Systems*, pages 161–171. ACM Press, New York.

[van den Bercken et al., 1997] van den Bercken, J., Seeger, B., and Widmayer, P. (1997). A generic approach to bulk loading multidimensional index structures. In *Proceedings of the 23rd International Conference on Very Large Databases (VLDB)*, pages 406–415.

[Venables and Ripley, 1994] Venables, W. N. and Ripley, B. D. (1994). *Modern Applied Statistics with S-Plus*. Springer Verlag, New York, Berlin.

[White and Jain, 1996] White, D. A. and Jain, R. (1996). Similarity indexing with the SS-tree. In *Proceedings of the 12th International Conference on Data Engineering, New Orleans*, pages 516–523.

[Wu and Buchmann, 1998] Wu, M.-C. and Buchmann, A. P. (1998). Encoded bitmap indexing for data warehouses. In *Proceedings of the 14th International Conference on Data Engineering (ICDE)*, pages 220–230.

[Yang et al., 1997] Yang, J., Karlapalem, K., and Li, Q. (1997). Algorithms for materialized view design in data warehousing environment. In *Proceedings of the 23rd International Conference on very Large Databases (VLDB)*, pages 136–145.

Index

Lecture Notes in Computer Science

For information about Vols. 1–2214
please contact your bookseller or Springer-Verlag